Play and Practice!

Play and Practice!

Graded games for English Language Teaching

Anthony Chamberlin
Kurt Stenberg

National Textbook Company
a division of *NTC Publishing Group* • Lincolnwood, Illinois USA

*Editions of this book are also
available from the following publishers: John Murray (United
Kingdom); Ernst Klett (West Germany); Librairie Belin
(France); Edizioni Scolastiche Bruno Mondadori (Italy);
Esselte Studium (Sweden); Munksgaard (Denmark);
Jacob Dijkstra (Netherlands); Dreyer (Norway); and
Otava (Finland).*

1996 Printing

5 6 7 8 9 ML 19 18 17 16 15 14 13 12 11

How to Use This Book

Play and Practice! has been compiled for teachers of English as a foreign or second language. It contains 98 games and provides for all levels, from absolute beginners to very advanced students.

These games are more than just relaxation. Some of them practice important grammatical structures, others train students in fluency. They offer teachers enjoyable ways of letting students practice what they have learned.

The book is divided into four main sections, each concentrating on one or more aspects of the main language skills. The aim of the games in the *Listen and Do* section is to test the students' understanding of spoken English and to check whether they are able to respond correctly to spoken commands. The games in the *Listen and Say* section demand both aural and oral skills. They range from guided pattern practice to free conversation. The *Reading and Writing* games deal with spelling, grammar, and fluency of expression. The *Social Games* are useful when English is to be practiced in an informal atmosphere and also outside the classroom. Within these main sections, games are arranged for quick reference in subsections such as "Words," "Structures," "General Comprehension," and "Fluency."

In order to help the teacher find a suitable game at a glance, there is a comprehensive table of contents at the beginning, as well as an index at the end of the book. The table of contents shows the nature of each game and the level for which it is best suited; the index lists the skills and items learned and refers to the games in which they may be practiced.

Level A assumes a limited vocabulary of nouns, mainly the names of everyday objects; a number of simple verbs; the forms of 'to be" and "to have" and a few basic sentence patterns; the ability to read and write English at an elementary level.

Level B assumes all forms of the present tense; questions and negative statements using the "do-don't" construction; the past tense and some irregular verbs; reading and writing in English.

Level C assumes all tenses and complex sentence patterns; a large general vocabulary; fluency in expression within the vocabulary and structures known.

Each game is preceded by a section that states the *Purpose* (the words and structures that are to be practiced), the *Language Required* (the necessary words and structures needed and sometimes the use of a hint as to the stage at which the game is best played), and *Preparation* (materials, practice, etc. that are needed to play the game—pictures, lists, cards, etc.). The *Game* gives a description of the game to be played as well as the rules. Often it will be necessary to use very simple language in describing the game to the students, and sometimes use of the students' dominant language will be inevitable. In the same way, the examples will frequently need to be adapted to the vocabulary and interests of the students.

Some of the games are competitions. This means that some students may be "out" at an early stage of the game. One way to prevent them from losing interest in the game is to give each player a number of "lives," perhaps from three to five, represented by books or pencils on his or her desk. A mistake then means that the student takes away one "life" but can still take part in the competition actively. Another possibility is that the student can regain a "life" by noticing and correcting the mistakes of others.

Each game is started by the teacher, but as soon as possible the leading role should go to the students. The teacher can then supervise the game, act as an umpire, and help those who may have any difficulties. Some games can be used for pair or group work, allowing the teacher to concentrate on helping one group at a time.

All the games described in this book have been played in language classes. They are easy to play, they work, and the students enjoy them. And—a most important point—they can and should be adapted to individual needs. This is a book of 98 suggestions, not 98 sets of unalterable rules.

A. C. & K. S.

vi

Contents

Listen and Say: Structures

Listen and Say: Conversation

1 Simon Says

Purpose *To practice listening comprehension by obeying simple commands.*

Language Required *In this game the students follow the teacher's actions. It is an excellent game for beginners as it gives them confidence in their ability to understand the language. They may not understand the words used, but will acquire vocabulary by watching the teacher's actions.*

Game This game can be used from the very first English lesson onwards. The rules are easy. The teacher stands in front of the class and gives an order for an action, beginning with the words "Simon says."He or she performs the action and tells the class to imitate him or her; but not to speak. Everything that "Simon says," the students must do.

    Simon says, "Hands up."
    Simon says, "Hands down."
    Simon says, "Thumbs up." etc.

Once the students get the idea of following the teacher's actions, the teacher explains that it is only when they hear "Simon says" that they should move. Otherwise they should sit still. If they make a mistake, they are "out"—that is to say, they must sit still until the end of the game. The winner is the student who is left doing what "Simon says" when all the rest have made a mistake.
The game goes like this:

    Simon says, "Fingers up."
All the students put their fingers up.
    "Fingers down."
The teacher puts his fingers down. Anyone who copies him is out.
    Simon says, "Fingers down."
All the students put their fingers down.
    "Hands up."
The teacher puts his hands up. Anyone who copies him is out. And so on until only one student is left.
Useful phrases to begin with:

Hands
Fingers   up/down.
Thumbs

Touch your eyes/ears/nose/mouth.
Put your hands on your heads/faces/knees.

Comments This basic form of the game has only a limited life, for students get better and better at it. After a while hardly anyone makes a mistake even when the commands are given very fast without allowing the players time to think. Here are two suggestions that will help to get students "out."

    Simon says, "Twiddle your thumbs."
    "Stop!" (Most players stop.)
The really unkind teacher—on a later occasion—asks, "Shall we play Simon says?"

    There is usually an enthusiastic shout of "Yes."
    Say, "All right, all stand up."
    Everyone stands up, everyone is out.
Warning When students realize they have been tricked, they may get very angry.

Alternatives In these games students no longer copy the teacher's movements; instead they listen and do as the teacher says. Consequently, the students must understand the orders given, and the alternatives should be played at a later stage.

(i) The teacher gives the commands without moving at all. The students should do as the teacher says, perhaps with their eyes shut, so they cannot copy each other.

(ii) The teacher says, "Touch your nose," but instead touches his ears. Anyone who touches his ears (as the teacher did) is out. It is possible to add the rule that anyone who plays with his eyes shut is out.

2　Express Delivery

Purpose *To practice listening comprehension, especially review of nouns, adjectives, and numbers.*

Language Required *A number of nouns (clothes, things in school, etc.), adjectives (colors, shapes, size, left, right, etc.), and numbers (1-10). The game can be adjusted by the teacher to suit known vocabulary.*

Preparation *Each team must have a stock of things handy; objects that you can usually find in the classroom should be enough.*

Game Goods which are required urgently are sent by *express delivery*. Similarly, the aim of this game is to obtain items as quickly as possible.

Divide the class up into four groups, one in each corner of the room. Put a desk or a chair in the middle of the classroom. Each group must have a "runner." The runner is the only person in the group who may leave his or her place and run to the middle of the room. The other members of the group must stay in their places, but they can, of course, give things to the runner.

The teacher asks for a number of objects, one at a time.

Examples　 a left shoe　　　 a scarf
　　　　　　a geography book　 a sweater
　　　　　　a letter　　　　　 a sock
　　　　　　five yellow pencils　a watch

The first runner to put the things on the chair or desk in the middle of the room gets a point for his or her team, and the team with the greatest number of points at the end of the game wins.

Comments Don't forget to make one person in each team the runner. By having a runner, you avoid having the whole class on the move at the same time. Ask for each object politely, using phrases like "I'd like a/Can I have a . . . please?"

3 Do It!

Purpose *To practice listening comprehension by obeying simple commands containing verbs of action or adjectives of mood or both.*

Language Required *Students should know various parts of the body (hands, fingers, thumbs, arms, head, etc.) and a number of verbs of action and adjectives of mood.*

Game The teacher gives commands without demonstrating the action. Students, either individually or as a group, must carry out the commands. Anyone making a mistake is "out." If the game is played as a competition between groups or teams, those who do the actions correctly get a point for their team.

Useful words and phrases:

walk (on the spot)	twiddle your thumbs
run (on the spot)	shut your eyes
jump	rub your nose
read	wave your hand
write	nod your head
sing	stand on your left/right foot
whistle	scratch your head

Among adjectives, those expressing mood can be useful, both for ordinary word training and as an introduction to using adjectives.

look happy	look angry	
look sad	look sleepy	etc.

Always start and finish with "Look happy."

Comment The game should be played quickly to test the students' command of verbs and adjectives. The more quickly they respond, the better they know the words.

4   In, On, Under

Purpose *To practice listening comprehension, especially prepositions of place.*

Language Required *Knowledge of prepositions of place and words for shapes (circle, square, etc.).*

Preparation *A sheet of paper for each student containing a few simple patterns. It can be a stencil or the students can copy the patterns themselves.*

Game Each student has a sheet of paper. It might look like this:

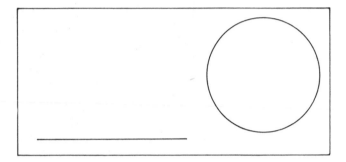

The teacher—or the leader—tells the students to do a number of things. For example:

    Put a cross in the circle.
    Write your name under the line.
    Write 4 to the left of the circle.

Students can easily correct their own sheets from a key the teacher shows them. The teacher can also collect the sheets and correct them for evaluation purposes.

There can be more shapes on the paper, and the shapes and commands can be more difficult, according to the ability of the students. For instance, one can use the outlines of familiar objects (a house, a car, a person) and ask the students to add details (windows, wheels, clothes) and neighboring objects (the sun, trees, etc.).

5 How Many Animals?

Purpose *To practice the recognition of nouns—in this example the names of animals, articles of clothing, and things in the classroom.*

Language Required *A number of nouns from each of the three areas mentioned above (or any other three the teacher chooses).*

Preparation *Each student needs a pencil and a piece of paper. The teacher prepares a list of words.*

Game Students divide their sheets of paper into three columns. One column is headed "Animals," one "Clothes," and one "Things in the classroom." If the class members have not started reading and writing, they can draw symbols instead, or write the headings in their own language. Show them on the blackboard the way the columns should look:

ANIMALS	CLOTHES	THINGS IN THE CLASSROOM

The teacher then reads out the names of a number of things that belong to one or other of the columns.

Examples   elephant   coat   chalk   desk
                    rabbit   dog   tie   etc.

The students mark each noun in the correct column like this:

ANIMALS	CLOTHES	THINGS IN THE CLASSROOM
/ / /	/ /	/ /

The teacher keeps count. After reading out a number of words, about 25 usually, he or she tells the students to count the numbers in each column and checks up to see if they have the correct totals.

    It need not be only the teacher who makes the list of words. One or more of the students can prepare a list and read it aloud.

Alternative When the students can write, they can write the words in the correct columns. Then, after the totals have been checked, they can see which of the words they misunderstood. Spelling can be checked, too. This is a dictation exercise, but slightly more interesting than usual.

6 Draw a Dog and Color it Brown

Purpose *To practice listening comprehension; the ability to understand oral instructions in English and to carry them out.*

Language Required *The students must know imperatives (draw, color, etc.), nouns for objects in and around the school, colors, adjectives like "small" and "big," some prepositions and prepositional phrases, and some simple sentence patterns.*

Preparation *Students need colored pencils or crayons and paper.*

Game The teacher or a selected student tells the class to draw a picture in stages, as follows:

Draw a tree in the middle of the paper.
Color the tree green.
Draw a black cat at the bottom of the tree.
Draw a bird at the top of the tree.
Draw another bird flying to the left of the tree.
Draw a yellow flower to the right of the cat.
And so on.

Check that the students' drawings are correct. If you wish, you can collect their drawings and then show them a drawing of your own.

Comments This game is quite easily adapted to classes at different levels. The instructions can vary from very short ones like "Draw a cat. Color it black," to long and complicated ones like "Draw a palm tree with a bird flying above it and a cat sleeping at the bottom."

Ambitious students may want to draw very detailed and complicated pictures. They should be taught to indicate what is to be in the picture and to finish it after the game.

7 Right or Wrong?

Purpose *To practice comprehension by labeling statements "Right" or "Wrong."*

Language Required *The words and structures used must be known by the students. The game can be adapted to any level of comprehension.*

Preparation *Make a list of suitable statements. Put two chairs by the blackboard and make sure there is space for students to run up to the chairs. Above one chair write "Right" and above the other "Wrong."*

Game Divide the class into two teams and number the players. Then make a statement, for example:

Queen Elizabeth is queen of the United States.

Pause, and then call a number: Five

The first number five to run out and sit—in this case on the "Wrong" chair—gets a point for his or her team.

Examples

Level A:	Level B:
We are playing a game now	We play football every Saturday
It's Friday today.	Los Angeles is in the north of the United States.
The sun is shining.	We are going to have a party tomorrow.
We all live in Dallas.	There are 52,000 inhabitants in our town.

Comments Passages from a textbook can also be used as a basis for this competition. The teacher prepares a number of statements that are right or wrong, according to a text that the students know. This can be a light-hearted way of checking homework.

Games where players move about are usually very popular. But if the teacher thinks that there is too much noise and movement, the students can remain in their seats and call out "That's right" or "That's wrong" instead. They can also mark their answers individually or in groups on an answer sheet.

Later on, at level C, a student or a group of students may take the teacher's place and read out prepared statements.

8 Yes or No?

Purpose *To practice recognition of vocabulary and common, simple question patterns.*

Language Required *This game can be adapted to any level of comprehension. The question patterns and words used must be known to the class.*

Preparation *Make a list of suitable questions of increasing difficulty. There must be about three times as many questions as there are students. The same questions can be used more than once.*

Game All the students have a number of "lives." Give them, say, four "lives" each, and let each one have four books on the desk to represent his or her "lives."

The teacher asks questions that demand "Yes" or "No" as an answer in an irregular fashion around the class. He or she should ask the questions quickly, giving students only a short time to think. If a student answers incorrectly, he or she loses a "life", and takes one of the books off the desk. By having several "lives," players do not drop out of the game too soon and, thus, lose interest. The winner is the player with most "lives" left at the end.

Examples of questions

Level A:

Is this a cat? (hold up a picture)
Can you speak English?
Is your English book blue?
Can you read Chinese?
Is three plus six eight?
Are there three lamps in the classroom?

Level B:

Are there 26 pupils in this class?
Do you go to school seven days a week?
Do we have a TV set at school?
Is New York a town in South America?
Are there lions in India?
Does John live in Florida?

Level C:

Does school finish in the second week of July?
Was the day before yesterday Sunday?
Did Napoleon live in the 17th century?
Do more than five million people live in Puerto Rico?

Comments The first time the game is played, the students need only answer "Yes" or "No." In this way the game tests their general comprehension. Later they can answer in short phrases."Yes, I can." "No, I can't." "Yes, I do." "No, he doesn't." "No, I didn't," etc. Played in this way, the game tests both general knowledge and structures.

Alternative If the teacher wants to test everyone in the class with the same questions, the students can write "Yes" or "No" on an answer sheet. In this case the questions must be numbered.

9   Who Is Who?

Purpose *To practice understanding oral descriptions of people and things.*

Language Required *The students should be fairly used to spoken English and know a number of words for things, colors, shapes, sizes, and positions.*

Preparation *Cut a number of pictures from newspapers, magazines, and catalogs, etc. The pictures should be large enough to be seen by all students from where they sit. Cut out, for example, 5 pictures of cars, 5 of men, 5 of women, 5 of dogs, etc. Letter each picture from (a) to (e).*

Game Choose one set of pictures and show it to the class. Describe one of the cars/men/women, etc. to the students and let them decide which of the pictures you are talking about. They answer orally with the appropriate letter, (a) to (e), or write the letter down. Alternatively, they can run up and point to the correct pictures, especially if you want to make a competition of the game. If the students write down the letter that they think is correct, you can evaluate how much each one has understood.

This game can be made easy or difficult, depending on the degree of similarity between the pictures and on the language used in the descriptions.

Once this game has been learned, a student can take over the job of describing a picture to a small group. The rest of the group guess which picture he or she is talking about.

10 Guide Me Through Town

Purpose *To practice following directions.*

Language Required *Phrases for finding the way must be practiced before the game.*

Preparation *Draw a map of a town, and give a copy to each student.*

Game When this game is used in its basic form, the teacher gives the directions, letting the students follow them on the map at the same time. It is important to agree upon a starting point.

Here is the sort of map you can draw yourself, and examples of the kinds of directions that might be given.

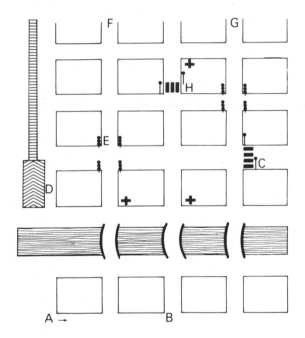

Start at point A.

Walk down the street. Turn left at the second corner, and walk up to the bridge. Turn right along the river. When you get to the next bridge, cross it. Walk up the street to the traffic lights. Turn left and then right at the next crossing. Where are you now?

You are at the corner marked H.

When you first practice this game, the students say where they are after the teacher has given the directions. Later it is possible to evaluate how well they can follow directions by asking them to write the letters for each position reached.

More advanced pupils can play the game in pairs or groups, giving each other instructions.

Alternative In order to practice the names of buildings and streets, you can name the different parts of the map: bank, post office, church, hospital, museum, school, etc. Thus, asking the way will be even more realistic, especially at level C.

11 "Say-the-Same" Game

Purpose *To practice pronunciation and the recognition of vowels and diphthongs.*

Language Required *A general vocabulary of at least a hundred words.*

Preparation *Groups of words containing the same vowel sound.*

Game The teacher pronounces very clearly a vowel sound that occurs in words the students have heard fairly frequently. To make the game easier, he or she can also give an example of a word with a vowel sound in it.

The students try to remember words with the same vowel sound and say the words. The teacher writes down every word as it is said so the class can say the words together afterwards. For example:

Teacher: [æ] (as in "cat")	Teacher: [ou] (as in "go")
Pupil 1: cat	Pupil 5: no
Pupil 2: hat	Pupil 6: home
Pupil 3: rat	Pupil 7: so
Pupil 4: bag	Pupil 8: stone
And so on.	And so on.

The class can be divided into teams and one point given for each correct word. In this case, there should be a time limit to speed up the game.

12   Train Noises

Purpose *To practice the ability to pronounce English words quickly and clearly.*

Language Required *The students need to know only a few hundred words which they can also pronounce correctly. The pronunciation of those phrases used must be practiced thoroughly before the game.*

Preparation *Find phrases or a rhyme containing the sounds you particularly want to practice. There are some suggestions below.*

Game If, for example, you talk about trains, write a menu for a dinner. Say that this is a dinner you can buy in the dining car of a train. The menu looks like this:

    Soup
    Fish and chips
    Peanut butter
    Cheese and biscuits
    Coffee

When this menu is said backwards—i.e., starting with coffee and finishing with the soup—it can sound like a train leaving a station. Say everything twice, except "Soup." Start very slowly and go faster and faster—the final "Soup" should sound like a whistle:

    Coffee, coffee
    Cheese and biscuits, cheese and biscuits
    Peanut butter, peanut butter
    Fish 'n chips, fish 'n chips
    SOUP

("Fish 'n chips" is said as fast as possible.)

When the whole class says it together (the teacher must keep time with his hand), the result is very effective.

Alternatives (i) Divide the class into two halves. One half says "Fish" with a long "ssshh," the other half says "Bacon and eggs." The teacher keeps time with his hand, and both halves speak at the same time:

    1   2
    Fisshh   Bacon and eggs
    Fisshh   Bacon and eggs
    And so on....

Go faster and faster until, when you can't say it any faster, everyone "whistles," that is to say, shouts "soup."

(ii) This old steam engine is panting up a hill. It goes slower and slower. The class say together:

I think I can, I think I can, . . .

It reaches the top and goes down the other side, going faster and faster:

I knew I could, I knew I could, . . .

Comments In classes where the teacher (or the students) do not enjoy singing, these "noises" can, to a certain extent, replace songs.

If you play the game at level C, let the students try to find rhythmic phrases themselves. They may show a lot of imagination and have great fun.

13   A Rhyming Game

Purpose *To practice comprehension of single words and the ability to choose words that rhyme from a limited vocabulary, and to pronounce the words correctly*

Language Required *A general vocabulary of at least 100 words.*

Game This game is not necessarily a competition. The teacher starts the game by saying, "I say *pen*," then he or she points to a student, who answers, "You say *pen*, and I say *hen*." This student then says, for example, "I say *head*," and points to another student, who might answer, "You say *head*, and I say *red*." And so on.

The students can put up their hands to show they know a word.

If the students are uncertain or slow, the teacher can help them by giving the first word all the time, thus making sure that they really know a word that rhymes.

Examples. Words that may be used:

    pen/hen/then/den/when/Ben/ten
    bed/head/Ned/red/said/Ted
    bike/hike/like
    ball/call/fall/hall/Paul/tall
    cat/fat/hat/mat/pat/rat
    book/cook/look/hook

14 Gossip

Purpose *Oral practice.*

Language Required *The game can be used as soon as students understand and use sentences of at least four words. Later it can be played at various different levels.*

Preparation *Think of a few "messages." At first they should be quite easy, but later on they can be more complicated.*

Game This is a whispering game that can be played along the rows in a classroom. The students who are sitting at the head of each row come to the front, and the teacher whispers a message to them. The message is usually a sentence, something like "I get up at seven and have ice cream for breakfast.

This sentence is then passed, in a whisper, along the row. Number one whispers it to number two, number two to number three, and so on. After the first practice round no student should be allowed to repeat the message a second time, even if the person he or she has whispered it to is uncertain what the message was. If a player is uncertain, he or she must repeat what he or she thinks the message was. When the message reaches the end of the rows, the last player can either write the message on the board or run out and whisper the message to the teacher.

Messages could perhaps be:

The table is beside the bed.
Come and see me on Tuesday next week.
Don't open the door—it's cold in here.
She says that she loves David.

Comments The students enjoy comparing their different results with the original sentence. It is amazing how the message sometimes changes, though perhaps not as drastically as in the old joke: A patrol of soldiers sent a whispered message back through the lines. "Send reinforcements, we are going to advance." When the message reached the officer, who was at the back, it ran, "Send three or four cents, we are going to a dance."

Alternative The game can be reversed: the last student in each row whispers a message to his or her neighbor and so on until it reaches the front. The student at the front whispers the message to the teacher who writes it on the board.

15   Arithmetic in Pairs

Purpose *To practice numbers in English.*

Language Required *Numbers up to at least 20 and the words "plus" and "minus."*

Preparation *Group students in pairs. A group of three is also possible.*

Game This is arithmetic, practiced in pairs and in English, instead of in the native language.

Give the students some examples on the board to show what is expected of them. Allow the examples to remain on the board for the weaker students to look at. Then start them off, letting them ask questions like:

What is two plus three?
What is four plus eight?
What is five minus four?
What is twelve minus eight?   etc.

The students should use full sentences: "What is two plus three?"—"It is five" (or only "Five"). "What is five minus four?"—"It is one." Etc.

Comments It is amazing how students who otherwise hate arithmetic (especially mental arithmetic) enjoy this game; this is particularly true of young students. They can communicate with each other in this simple way without the teacher's help. The game is very good for practicing pair work—even after only a few weeks of English.

16   Buzz

Purpose   *To practice numbers in English.*

Language Required   *Some training in numbers.*

Game   In this game the class counts aloud, each player saying one number in turn, but every time students come to a seven, they must say "buzz" instead of the number. They say it for all numbers containing a seven—7, 17, 27, 71, 72, etc....and also for all numbers that are multiples of seven—14, 21, 28, etc.

The counting goes:

1, 2, 3, 4, 5, 6, buzz, 8, 9, 10, 11, 12, 13, buzz, 15, 16, buzz, 18, 19, 20, buzz, 22, 23, 24, 25, 26, buzz, buzz, 29, 30, etc. . . .

Anyone who makes a mistake is out.

Comments   The game is less successful in a large class. Once students are out, they lose interest in the game and may start talking. Two ways of retaining interest are as follows. Start again at one as soon as someone is out. This means that the class does not usually reach high numbers which are difficult to follow (but it is often the high numbers that need to be practiced). Or else give everyone two or three "lives."

Three and multiples of three can be used instead of seven.

"Buzz" is not a very useful sound. Nevertheless, it is traditional for this game. But why not practice a word such as "toothbrush" or "tomato" and say that instead of "buzz"? Or, let the pupils say any English word they like, perhaps beginning with a certain letter.

17 Throwing the Dice

Purpose *To practice numbers in English.*

Language Required *Numbers from 1—50 or 1—100; "plus" and "minus."*

Preparation *Get one or more dice. One die is needed for each group.*

Game Each group of students is given a die. The first student throws the die. He or she says out loud what is on the die, for example, "Three." He or she passes the die to the next person who throws it and says, for example, "Two." He or she adds this score to the previous score and then says aloud, "Two plus three is five." He or she passes the die on. The next one says, for example, "Four—four plus five is nine" and, in turn, passes the die on.

The group—or row—with the highest or lowest total wins.

Alternatives (i) A certain number, six for example, can be regarded as a minus number which must be subtracted from the previous total.

(ii) Another idea is to let each team start with one hundred from which they must subtract each number that they throw. For example, number one throws five. He or she says, "Five. A hundred minus five is ninety-five." The die is then passed to number two, and so on. This is a way of practicing higher numbers.

18 Twenty-one

Purpose *To practice numbers in English.*

Language Required *Numbers up to at least 21.*

Preparation *Group the students in pairs. A group of three is possible.*

Game There are two players and they agree that the one who says a number—21, for example—wins. They take turns saying one or two numbers. They can't say more than two numbers, which must be in sequence.

Example:

Player 1:	1	2	Player 2:	10	11
Player 2:	3		1:	12	
1:	4		2:	13	14
2:	5	6	1:	15	16
1:	7		2:	17	18
2:	8		1:	19	20
1:	9		2:	21	

In this case number 2 wins, as he or she is the one who says "21."

Comments Change the winning numbers; do not always start with 1. In this way you avoid saying the same numbers all the time. Start at 30, for example, and make 55 the winning number. The numbers can also be counted backwards, starting from 21, 50, or 100, the winner ending with 1.

Look at game 20 to see how this can be played with letters instead of numbers.

19   Number Bingo

Purpose *To practice understanding numbers in English.*

Language Required *Numbers from 1—50 or 51—100, depending on vocabulary.*

Preparation *Bingo "stencils" for each student and a set of numbered "counters." Of course, a set of bingo cards can be bought instead.*

Game Give each player a bingo "card." It might look like this:

				1-10
				11-20
				21-30
				31-40
				41-50

The players then fill in their cards, choosing any four numbers they like between 1 and 10 to put in the top four squares, any four numbers between 11 and 20 in the four squares in the second row, etc. The teacher can always fill in the cards before giving them to the students.

The teacher, or a student, draws the numbered counters out of a hat or a bag, and calls out the number. Any player with that number on his or her card crosses it off.

Give the first prize to the first player with a complete horizontal or vertical line crossed off.

Give the next prize to the first player with a complete card crossed off. The teacher should check that the card is correct—if the counters are arranged in order on the teacher's desk as they are called out, it is easy to do this.

Traditionally, the player who wins should shout "Bingo," but players can shout instead, "I've got a line" or "My card's full."

Comments In order to practice the numbers themselves, the students may take turns calling out the numbers.

20 The Alphabet in Pairs

Purpose *To practice the letters of the alphabet.*

Language Required *The alphabet in English.*

Game There are two players, and they agree that the one who says a letter—M, for example—wins. They then take turns saying one or two letters of the alphabet, but no more.

Example

Player 1:	A	
Player 2:	B	C
1:	D	E
2:	F	G
1:	H	
2:	I	
1:	J	K
2:	L	M

In this case, player 2 wins for saying "M."

Comment Change the winning letter; don't always start with "A." In this way, all the letters of the alphabet can be practiced.

The game is good for practicing the alphabet in English with younger students. With older students it can be used as a social game.

Game 18 shows how to play with numbers instead of letters.

21 Good Morning, Susan

Purpose *To practice greetings such as "Good morning," "Good afternoon," "How are you?" etc., or, in the alternative game, polite conversational phrases.*

Language Required *A number of phrases, such as "Good morning," etc. See below.*

Game Susan—for example—goes to the front of the classroom, shuts her eyes, and turns her back to the class. The teacher points to one of the students who says, "Good morning, Susan." Susan must reply "Good morning, David"—if she thinks it was David who spoke. If she is right, she and David change places. If she is wrong, another student says "Good morning"—or some other phrase of greeting—perhaps choosing one from a list that has been written on the blackboard. The game continues until Susan guesses correctly who it was that spoke.

Other useful phrases:

How do you do?	Good morning.	Good night.
Goodby.	Good afternoon.	Hello.
How are you?	Good evening.	

Comments Students can move from their seats to another part of the room before they speak. They can also disguise their voices.

Alternative At a more advanced stage, students can use other conversational phrases which must then be answered appropriately, using the name of the supposed speaker.

Examples

Hello, Susan. How are you?
Fine, thanks, and how are you, David?
Nice weather today, isn't it?
Yes, David, it's lovely.

22 What Color is Henry's Shirt?

Purpose *To practice colors.*

Language Required *The names of classroom objects, clothes, and colors.*

Preparation *Possibly some review of nouns.*

Game When practicing colors, teachers usually ask about the color of objects in the room. This is much more fun if all the students have their eyes shut. The teacher can ask the color of things in the room or of students' shirts and sweaters. Or of his or her own clothes—the students hardly ever seem to know.

Teacher: What color is Henry's shirt, Mary?
Mary: It is blue.
Teacher: Yes, that's right./No, guess again.
And so on.

Comments Students get so interested in this game that they "cheat" and open their eyes if they don't know the answer.

If you want to use students' trousers, shoes, and socks as objects, they must be familiar with the plural, "They are black," etc.

23 I Spy

Purpose *To practice the names of objects in and around the classroom, or in pictures.*

Language Required *The alphabet should be well known: nouns; the phrases "Yes, it is" and "No, it isn't."*

Game When children play this game, they say, "I spy, with my little eye, something beginning with (for instance) D." The others try to guess what it is:

Is it a door?—No, it isn't.
Is it a desk?—No, it isn't.
Is it a dress?—Yes, it is.

The person who guesses correctly then "spies" the next thing, which must easily be seen from his or her seat.

Instead of using the classroom and the things that can be seen outside the window, pictures can be used. In this way you can practice words from a certain subject area, for instance, the garden, a street in town, or a grocery store. Words from a textbook can be practiced if there are good illustrations.

Comment Instead of "I spy, with my little eye," it is possible to use the easier phrase, "I can see something beginning with . . . " or "I spy something beginning with . . . "

24　Kim's Game

Purpose *To practice nouns and, in the alternative game, prepositions of place.*

Language Required *Some knowledge of names of objects that can be found in the classroom and of prepositions of place.*

Game The game, a memory game, is called "Kim's Game" because it was described by Rudyard Kipling in the book *Kim*.

Let the students look at a number of objects. Fifteen or twenty objects are about the right number. The objects can be real ones on a desk, drawings on the blackboard, or pictures on the flannel board.

After one minute, the objects are taken away or covered. The students try to remember all the objects. They say what they can remember, or they can make a written list.

Comment If you use real objects on a desk, you must remember that not all students will be able to see clearly. Let the class come to the front in groups, one group at a time, and then go back to their desks to write their lists.

Alternatives (i) In this version students try to remember the *position* of the objects.

The teacher can ask:

Where is the knife?

The students answer:

Between the red pencil and the ruler.

And so on.

(ii) Put a number of things on the desk, as before. The students shut their eyes. Move one of the objects. The students open their eyes and try to see which object has been moved. They say, for example:

The pencil was between the book and the glass; now it is to the right of the bag.

or

The knife was under the cup; now it is in the glass.

25 I'm Going to Boston

Purpose *To practice nouns and the pronunciation of the names of towns in English-speaking countries. In the alternative game the aim is to practice adjectives and nouns.*

Language Required *Students should have some knowledge of the names of towns in the English-speaking world, and should know a fair number of nouns and adjectives.*

Preparation *A geography lesson might be useful shortly before the game is to be played in order to review the names of towns.*

Game This game can be played either by two teams or in pairs. Team one, or number one in the pair, thinks of a town and says, for example, "I'm going to Boston." The other team—or person—then asks, "Please buy me some beans," choosing something that starts with the same letter as the town.

Other examples:

Team 1: I'm going to New York.
Team 2: Please buy me some nuts.
Team 2: I'm going to Los Angeles.
Team 1: Please buy me some lamps.

And so on.

Change each time, so that the team that asked for something names a town the next time. Allow no more than ten seconds for a team to think of a town or something to buy.

Scoring: One point for a town, one point for something you can buy.

Both towns and articles must be given a sentence:

I'm going to . . .
Please buy me some . . .

Comment Students must choose towns in English-speaking countries.

Alternative In order to practice adjectives and add to the difficulty of the game, each noun can be preceded by an adjective starting with the same letter as the noun. The examples above could then become:

Please buy me some baked beans.
Please buy me some nice nuts.
Please buy me some lovely lamps.

26 The Baker's Cat

Purpose *To practice adjectives.*

Language Required *Students should know enough adjectives to be able to cover most of the alphabet.*

Game This game can be played in two teams or in pairs. It consists of finding an adjective to describe the baker's cat. The first adjective must begin with "A," the second with "B," the third with "C," and so on. Either a player uses the next consecutive letter when his or her turn comes, or each letter may be used twice.

Example

The baker's cat is an African cat.
The baker's cat is a beautiful cat.
The baker's cat is a crazy cat.
The baker's cat is a dirty cat.

It is a good idea to let each team choose the first adjective alternately—it is fairer that way.

Scoring: 1 point for each adjective.

Comments It is probably best to leave out X and Z and perhaps one or two other letters.

The word "baker" can, of course, be changed. The game can be called "My aunt's cat" instead.

27 What Can You Do with an Apple

Purpose *To practice verbs.*

Language Required *Students should have a stock of about a hundred verbs to choose from.*

Game The game can be played either in groups or individually.

The leader, teacher or student, asks a question, for example, "What can you do with an apple?" The students (groups) then say one or more sentences, as many as they have time for in, perhaps, 15 seconds.

An obvious answer would be, "You can eat it," but other answers must, of course, be correct, such as, "You can make jam with it," "You can cook it," "You can throw it," "You can sell it," etc.

Give one point for each acceptable suggestion.

Other words

brick	car	letter
bed	one dollar	match
stone	book	fish
cat	telephone	shoe

Comment Sometimes it is possible to choose key words (those for things you can do something with, e.g. "apple") that fit together with verbs learned earlier.

28 Word Pairs

Purpose *To practice using words with the same pronunciation and different meanings.*

Language Required *The students should be able to build proper sentences and be used to building sentences around given words.*

Preparation *Sometimes it is necessary to give some initial training in word pairs with the same pronunciation.*

Game One player, or a team, thinks of two words that are either spelled the same—for example, *box* (something to keep things in) and *box* (to fight)—or else spelled differently but pronounced the same—for example, *meet* and *meat*. Team 1 then makes up one or two sentences containing the words, but says (or writes) *sausage* instead of the words. The other team tries to guess the correct words.

Examples

When the two men started to **sausage,** the cat was so frightened it jumped into a **sausage** to hide. (box)

I must go into town to buy **sausage,** so you can **sausage** me outside the butcher's. (meat; meet)

Other words

tale; tail	blue; blew	pair; pear
bare; bear	hair; hare	right; write
lean (thin); lean	break; brake	sea; see
piece; peace	son; sun	light; light
cross (the street); cross (angry)	one; won	would; wood

29   I Went to Town

Purpose *To practice listening comprehension, the names of things you can buy, and the use of "a," "an," and "some."*

Language Required *Thorough knowledge of the verbal forms "went" and "bought," a wide vocabulary of names of things you can buy, and the use of "a," "an," and "some."*

Game This is a memory game. The first player starts by thinking of something that he or she could buy in the village. He or she says:

I went to town and bought some eggs.

Then it is the second player's turn. He or she adds something, saying:

I went to town and bought some eggs and some tomatos.

The next player adds another item:

I went to town and bought some eggs, some tomatos, and an ice cream cone.

And so it goes until someone makes a mistake.

Comments Write down a list of what the students buy as the game goes on. Otherwise it is so easy to forget the things yourself.

You can play this game with small groups. In a large class you cannot expect to get to everyone before someone forgets something. An alternative is to have teams of between five and ten players and to start from the beginning with each team. Give one point for every member who remembers the list and five extra points if the whole team remembers it.

Alternative If you want to practice certain subject areas, you can also say, "I went to the bakery/grocery store/toy store/record store/department store," etc.

30 Do You Have a Pencil in Your Hand?

Purpose *To practice nouns with "Do you have...?" and "Yes, I do," "No, I don't."*

Language Required *The names of objects that are to be used during the game and how to use "Do you have?" and "Does he(she) have?"*

Preparation *A number of small objects must be available in the classroom.*

Game This is a very popular guessing game—one student holds something hidden in his or her hands, and the others try to guess what it is.

It often takes a long time for the students to guess correctly. The way to avoid this difficulty is to limit the number of objects to about five or six. Let the class see all the objects and then hide them in a drawer, under your desk, or on a chair outside the classroom. One student goes forward, chooses one of the objects, and hides it in his or her hands.

Do you have a ball in your hand?
No, I don't.
Do you have a pencil in your hand?
Yes, I do.

Whoever guesses correctly chooses the next object. In this way the number of objects—and guesses—is limited and the game moves quickly.

Alternatives (i) Put the objects on a chair in the hall. Place a hat beside the objects. Player 1 goes out, chooses an object, puts it on his or her head, and then hides it by putting on the hat. When player 1 comes back into the classroom, the class tries to guess what is under the hat.

Do you have a mouse under your hat?
No, I don't.
Do you have a pencil under your hat?
Yes, I do.

The game proceeds accordingly. Note that if young students are playing, be sure that the objects do not have points, sharp edges, etc.

(ii) The game is also suitable for practicing the third person form: "Does he have an eraser on his head?" or "Does she have a crayon under her hat?" Two students work together, one of them hiding the object and the other answering questions about what is hidden.

31 What Do I Have in My Bag?

Purpose *Question and answer practice using the patterns "You have..." and "Do you have?" (In the alternative game the "has" form is used)*

Language Required *Use nouns familiar to the students who should have learned the two constructions. (In alternative, "He has"/"Does she have.")*

Preparation *Put in a large bag a number of small objects whose names the pupils know.*

Game This game applies the pattern drill to a situation, making it more interesting.

The teacher takes a large, interesting-looking bag or basket into the classroom. When he or she shakes it, perhaps it makes a strange noise. The teacher says, "What do I have in my bag?" The students try to guess:

Do you have a horse in your bag?
Do you have a car in your bag?
Do you have a doll in your bag?

Every time the teacher answers "Yes, I do," he or she takes the object out of the bag and puts it on the desk.

After all the things have come out of the bag, the class can talk about them for a few minutes.

What's this?—What color is it?—Is it big or small—Do you have a book on your desk, too?

Then the teacher puts everything back in the bag. The pattern now becomes a memory game—"Well, what *do* I have in my bag?"

The pupils answer orally:
You have a horse and a mouse and a car.
Good. Now you, Mary.
You have a knife and a doll and . . ..
Good. And Peter.
You have a hat and a book.

And so on until the students have named all the objects in the bag.

Comments Have one or two new objects in the bag to add interest—for instance, a toy animal the students have not seen before.

The teacher can also point out to the students the different intonation used when asking the question, "Do you have...?" and when making a statement, "You have..."

Alternative To practice the construction "Does he (she) have....?", let a student come to the front and look in the bag. The other students can then ask questions as above, saying for example:

Does she have a horse in her bag?
Does she have a car in her bag?   etc.

32   What Is He Doing?

Purpose *To practice the present continuous singular form of common verbs, first in the third person, then, in the alternative, in the first and second persons.*

Language Required *A thorough knowledge of twenty to thirty verbs and constructions using the present continuous tense. The first and second persons may be practiced separately as an alternative or all three combined.*

Game A student comes to the front and mimes a little scene; that is, he or she "acts" without saying anything. The actor pretends, perhaps, that he or she is getting up in the morning. The rest of the class tries to guess what the actor is doing. The class asks the teacher or another student:

Is he riding a bike?

The teacher, or student, answers:

No, he isn't.
Is he reading?
No, he isn't.

And so on until they guess:

Is he getting up?
Yes, he is.

Then another student comes to the front. At first the teacher whispers to the actor what he or she is to do. For example:

Drink a glass of water.
Ride a bike.
Drive a car.

Later the students can decide what to do themselves. Some suggestions for actions:

Get up in the morning		football	Ride a skateboard
Drive a car		tennis/golf	Iron your clothes
Go to bed	Play	basketball	Clean the windows
Ride a horse		the trumpet	Paint a picture
Ride a bike		the piano	Sell hot dogs

Alternative This game can also be used to practice the first and second person singular. The questions are put directly to the student who is doing the mime:

Are you driving a car?
No, I'm not.
Are you reading?
No, I'm not.
Are you getting up?
Yes, I am.

33 What Is There in the Bag?

Purpose *To practice the question "Is there....?," or "Are there....?," with appropriate intonation.*

Language Required *Names of common objects and knowledge of "Is there?" and "Are there?"*

Preparation *A number of objects and a bag. If the alternative is to be played, there must be two or more of each object.*

Game Show the students a number of objects. Then hide them—put them on a chair behind the teacher's desk, for example. One student comes to the front, takes one of the objects, and puts it in a bag. The others try to guess what is in the bag.

Is there a ball in the bag?
No, there isn't.
Is there a tiger in the bag?
No, there isn't.
Is there a monkey in the bag?
Yes, there is.

The student who guesses correctly comes to the front, takes the object out of the bag, and chooses another object to put in.

Alternative To practice the plural form "Are there . . . ," use two or more objects of the same kind. First play the game in the singular only, then in the plural only, then with the singular and the plural mixed. At this last stage the game becomes much more difficult.

Comment Always be careful to practice intonation in the questions *before* the game starts. It will ruin the fun if you have to interrupt the students to correct their intonation.

34 Hunt the Thimble

Purpose *To practice prepositions of place—in, on, under, behind, in front of, over there, to the left of, etc.—and to practice asking questions.*

Language Required *Names of things in the classroom should be well known, question forms should be familiar, and prepositions of place previously learned.*

Game This is a classroom variant of the party game of the same name. When you play the game in the classroom, one student goes out and another hides the thimble (or a pencil). When the student who has been outside comes in again, he or she may ask fifteen questions in order to try to find the thimble. He or she may only ask questions that can be answered by "Yes" or "No."

Example

    Am I near the thimble now?
    Is it over there?
    Is it in a desk?
    Is it under a book?
    Do you have the thimble?
    Is it at the front of the room?
    Is it behind you?
    Can you see it?

You can time the players to see how quickly they find the thimble.

To avoid a silent game, with the student looking and not asking anything, write a number of questions on the blackboard. If the student says nothing, point to one of the questions, and make him or her ask that particular question.

Alternative Send out two or more students who represent different teams. Put several things around the room in places where they can be seen. The students are called in from outside and told what they are looking for. As soon as a player has seen all the things, he or she sits down. When everyone is sitting down, ask the first one who sat down where the things are. If he or she is wrong, ask the second one who sat down, and so on.

35 The King Likes Tea, But He Doesn't Like Coffee

Purpose *To practice the third person singular of verbs ending in "-s" and the negative "doesn't."*

Language Required *To be able to play the game at a fair speed, the students need to know a number of nouns. They should also know the third person in "-s" and the "doesn't" construction.*

Game The king lives in a strange land. Some things he likes; some things he doesn't like. Give a list to the children, for instance:

The king likes white,	but he doesn't like black.
cats,	dogs.
Saturday,	Sunday.

Then the students suggest statements:

Example

Student: The king likes cars, but he doesn't like bicycles.

Teacher (or one of the students who knows the secret):
No, that's wrong. The king doesn't like cars, and he doesn't like bicycles.

Student: The king likes tigers, but he doesn't like elephants.

Teacher: No, that's wrong. The king likes tigers, and he likes elephants.

After a while you can tell the pupils the secret. The king likes "T," meaning words that contain the letter "T." Don't tell the secret too early. Once they know how to play the game, the students can continue, perhaps writing sentences to practice spelling.

Alternatives There are many varieties of this game. Another letter—"I" perhaps—being the key rather than "T." Or, the game can be played so that a word must begin with the first letter of the name of the person who is speaking. Another phrase can be used such as:

When I went to Mexico, I took . . .

Example

Mary: When I went to Mexico, I took a model.

Brian: When I went to Mexico, I took a box.

Peter: When I went to Mexico, I took a case.

Teacher: No, Peter, that's wrong.

Comment This alternative is *very* frustrating.

36   What Do You Do?

Purpose *To practice "Do you . . . ?", "Does he (she) . . . ?" etc. with the appropriate answers.*

Language Required *Previous knowledge of the construction with which the game is played.*

Game This game is best played in pairs. Each person chooses one sentence out of a number given on the board. Here are some examples.

I like pudding.
I always go to bed before 10 o'clock.
I watch TV every day.
I sometimes eat candy at school.
I play baseball.
I drive a car.
I walk to school.
I eat apples.   etc.

In each pair, one person asks a question. The other answers it and then asks a question of his or her own. The aim is to discover which sentence one's partner has chosen, i.e., what he or she does. The winner is the one who guesses correctly first.

1:   Do you like pudding?
2:   No, I don't.—Do you drive a car?
1.   No, I don't.—Do you play baseball?
2.   No, I don't.—Do you like pudding?
1.   Yes, I do.—What do you do?
2.   I walk to school.

To avoid cheating, each student should write the sentence he or she has chosen on a piece of paper.

Alternative If you want to practice the third person, "Does he like pudding?", divide the class into groups of three. Number 1 starts by whispering his or her chosen activity to number 2. Number 3 then asks all the questions, and number 2 answers them. After the correct activity has been guessed, number 2 chooses an activity and whispers it to number 3 who has to answer all the questions from number 1. The third round of the game starts by number 3 choosing an activity, and so on. The winner is the one who guesses, using the least number of questions.

37 What Did You Buy?

Purpose *To practice the past tense of irregular verbs.*

Language Required *The students should be able to ask and answer questions in the past tense. They should know a number of irregular verbs and some adjectives.*

Game The teacher, or a student, asks a question using an irregular verb. The answer given must contain at least one word that starts with the same letter as the verb in the past tense. For example:

What did you buy?
I bought a book.
When did you go to the zoo?
I went on Wednesday.
Who did you see?
I saw Susan.

When the students are familiar with the way the game is played, they can work in pairs.

The game can be made more difficult by asking for two or three words in the answer starting with the same letter as the verb. For example;

What did you buy?
I bought a brown book.
When did you go to the zoo?
I went on Wednesday last week.
Who did you see?
I saw Susan, standing in the street.   etc

38   A Verb Game

Purpose   *To practice verbs, stating the tense or tenses to be used.*

Language Required   *Some previous practice of verb forms and tenses is desirable.*

Game   This game can be played between the teacher and the class, in pairs, or between two teams. The first time the game is played, it is most successful between teacher and class.

First, the class must decide what tense to use during the game, the simple past, for example.

The teacher starts off by saying:

You had a book, Mary.

Mary then says what she did with the book, using a verb in the correct tense, for example:

I opened the book.

The teacher then goes on making statements to students who respond in the same way as Mary in the example above.

Here are some examples:

You had a bike.	I rode to school.
Tom had a canoe.	He paddled in the river.
Ann had a net.	She caught fish.
We had a big ball.	We played football.
They had a car.	They drove it.

When the students are fairly advanced, the teacher can mix tenses during the game.

In the earlier stages it may be wiser to stick to one person of the verb (third person) at a time. The student who can carry on the longest without making a mistake is the winner.

When the students have gotten used to the game, they can play it in pairs, which is perhaps the best way of playing it. The students challenge each other, agree upon a tense (and person), and give the key phrase alternately.

If one student cannot produce a reasonable verb, he or she may challenge his or her opponent to do so. If the latter cannot do so, he or she loses a point. If the opponent can, the challenger loses one.

If the game is played as a competition between two teams, the members of each team should be numbered. Then the game would run:

A1	Tom has a ball.	B1	He bounces it.
B1	Tom has a train.	A2	He plays with it.
A2	Tom has a room.	B2	He sleeps in it.
B2	Tom has a glass.	A3	He breaks it.

And so on, until the last member of team B has made a statement.

Comment If the game is a competition between two teams, the teacher must keep the score and make decisions very quickly if disputes arise.

39   Who Am I?

Purpose *To practice the question forms "Are you . . . ?" and "Do you . . . ?" and the answers, "Yes, I am," "No, I'm not," "Yes, I do," and "No, I don't."*

Language Required *Knowledge of the constructions; words for different nationalities, activities, professions, etc.*

Game This is a variant of "20 questions." A member of the class comes to the front and thinks of a well-known person. The rest of the class try to guess who the person is. The student at the front answers questions—up to 20—but he or she only answers:

Yes, I am.
No, I'm not.
Yes, I do.
No, I don't.

Class:	Are you Swedish?
Student:	No, I'm not.
Class:	Are you American?
Student:	No, I'm not.
Class:	Are you Japanese?
Student:	Yes, I am.
Class:	Do you play football?
Student:	No, I don't.
Class:	Are you a sports star?
Student:	Yes, I am. etc.

If the correct answer is found with 20 questions or fewer, the class wins. Otherwise the student at the front wins. The teacher, or one of the students, must keep count of the questions.

The first time this game is played, it is a good idea to write a number of questions on the board to start the game off. There are also a few words—-"sports star," "movie star," "politician," etc.—that the class will need. You can write something like this:

Are you Japanese/Swedish/American/German?
Are you a man/a woman?
Are you young/old?
Are you alive/dead?
Do you live in Tokyo/Hollywood/Paris?
Are you a sports star/movie star/politician?
Do you play football/ice hockey/tennis?

Comments One way of making this game slightly easier is to decide that the pupils must think of someone who has been discussed recently in class—not necessarily in English lessons. Another way is to give the initial of the surname.

Alternative Instead of the class asking one of the students and trying to guess who he or she is, the game can be played the other way round. One student goes out and the class decides who he or she is. The "guesser" then comes in again and asks questions to which the class answers "Yes" or "No." Again, the limit is 20 questions.

1: Am I Puerto Rican?
2: Yes, you are.
1: Do I live in New York?
3: No, you don't.   etc.

The great advantage of playing the game this way is that everyone must be prepared to answer a question.

40 What Have You Done?

Purpose *To practice the perfect tense of common verbs.*

Language Required *The students should know enough verbs, nouns, and prepositions to be able to talk about simple actions in the classroom.*

Preparation *Some review of tenses might be needed before the game is played.*

Game One student comes to the front of the class so that everybody can have a look at him or her. Then that student goes out of the room. While outside, he or she does something to change appearance. When the student has come in again, the class tries to guess what he or she has done—it should be something they can see.

Have you combed your hair?
Have you buttoned/unbuttoned your shirt?
Have you taken off your ring?
Have you put your left shoe on your right foot?
Have you washed your hands?

Comment Suggest about six or seven things that a student could do, at least the first time you play the game.

Examples

Take off your watch.
Take off your hair ribbon.
Pull your handkerchief half out of your pocket.
Take off your left/right sock.
Take your bracelet off your left arm and put it on your right arm.
Tie up/untie your shoe lace.
Put your left shoe on your right foot.   etc.

41   She Went to the Blackboard

Purpose *To practice the simple past of some common verbs.*

Language Required *Knowledge of verbs for actions that can be carried out in the classroom, the imperative, and the simple past.*

Preparation *Make a list of the verbs you want the students to practice.*

Game Choose a "runner" and let the students give him or her orders, using imperative forms from a list of verbs written on the blackboard.

Example

> Go to the blackboard; write your name; erase it; draw a cat; go to the piano; play a song; go back to your seat; sit down.

The class watches him or her all the time and tries to remember what he or she has done. After the runner has finished, the teacher asks:

> What did he (or she) do?

Now the class tries to give an accurate account of what the runner did—in the correct order.

> She went to the blackboard, wrote her name, erased it, drew a cat, . . .

Comment If you want to make a competition out of it, divide the class into groups of three to five, and give them some time to put together an oral report. Then walk round and listen to the answers. One point for each correct verb, five extra points if all are correct in form as well as in pronunciation.

Alternative The game can also be played by two teams. Team A gives the runner a fixed number of orders, perhaps 8 or 10. Team B must give an account of what the runner did. Then Team B gives the orders and team A must report the actions.

42   What Would You Do?

Purpose *To practice conversational use of the conditional "would."*
Language Required *The students must have some fluency in spoken English and must understand and be able to use "would."*
Preparation *Make a list of situations which the students might be able to talk about.*

Game One student goes out. The rest of the class decides on a difficult situation. The student outside the door is in that difficult situation and must try to guess what it is. Perhaps he or she has just eaten at a restaurant and has no money. The student then comes in again and asks "What would you do?" to as many others in the class as necessary. They must answer, telling what they would do in the situation, but without telling what the situation is. Their answers might be like this:

1: Mary, what would you do?
2: I would try to borrow some money.
1: What would you do, John?
3: I would call my parents.
1: What would you do, David?
4: I would look in my pockets again.
1: Carol, what would you do?
5: I would wash dishes for the rest of the evening.   etc.

The student who has been outside must try to guess the difficult situation he or she is in, using as few questions as possible.

Difficult situations that could be used:

You are up a tree with an angry bull underneath.
A waiter just dropped a bowl of soup in your lap.
Your girl friend/boy friend calls when you are with another boy/girl.
Your trousers start to fall down.
You are hanging by your hands over a cliff.
You are driving a car. The brakes do not work.
You want to knock on someone's door, but a dog is standing in front of it, barking at you.

43   Hide-and-Seek in a Picture

Purpose *To practice names of objects in a house and prepositions.*

Language Required *Names of objects and rooms in a house, and at least the prepositions "in," "on," "under," and "behind." Question form, "Are you . . . ?"*

Preparation *You need a picture of a house, preferably one showing several rooms. One that you can put up on the wall or show on an overhead projector is best, but a blackboard drawing or a textbook illustration would do.*

Game One student "hides" in the picture. He or she chooses a hiding place and imagines that he or she is hidden there—behind the clock in the dining room, for example, or under the table in the kitchen. The other class members try to guess where he or she is hidden by asking questions which can be answered with "Yes" or "No."

Examples

> Are you upstairs?
> Are you in the dining room?
> Are you behind the chair?
> Are you under the table?

You may limit the number of questions to ten so that as many students as possible have turns. The student who guesses the hiding place correctly then "hides."

Comment The student should tell the teacher beforehand where he or she has hidden, in case help is needed during the game.

44 Where's the Fly?

Purpose *To practice prepositions of place and direction.*

Language Required *A knowledge of relevant prepositions and the names of objects in a room.*

Preparation *You will need a picture of a furnished room to put up on the wall or blackboard or to show on an overhead projector. You can also use a picture in a textbook or the classroom itself.*

Game The teacher is the guide and everybody in the class the fly. Without pointing at the picture the teacher (the guide) says, for example:

> Come in under the bottom of the door. Fly up the wall, across the ceiling to the lamp, down onto the table, across the room to the dresser. Fly into the open drawer, see what is in it. Fly out of the drawer, around the vase and in behind the picture on the wall.
> Where are you?

The students (the flies) try to follow the directions. When they hear the question, they answer, for example:

> I'm behind the picture on the wall.

The game can be repeated several times. Start with short directions and make them gradually longer and more complicated.

When the students are fairly good at the game, they can play it in twos. Then they alternate between being the guide and the fly. Limit the number of directions to five or seven.

Comment If all the students have a copy of the picture (for instance, if you use a picture in a textbook), they can trace the fly's route with a pencil. Use different colors to follow the fly's different routes. The route can be checked between each "journey."

45　A Ship in a Fog

Purpose *To be able to give and obey simple commands involving movement in different directions.*

Language Required *Previous training in words for direction.*

Preparation *Plenty of space is needed to place obstacles between the starting point and the goal. These should not be too close together. A school playground, hall, or gymnasium is suitable. As obstacles you can use such things as desks, chairs, boxes, piles of books, or even students. A scarf is needed for blindfolding (optional).*

Game The object of this game is for one student, the Captain, to guide a blindfolded* colleague, the Ship, to a Port, using verbal instructions to steer the Ship round the obstacles. The Port can be an opening between two chairs into which the Ship must go after completing the journey. The Captain can give such commands as:

One step forward.
One small step to the right.
Three steps forward.
Stop.
Two steps to the left.
A small step backwards.
Turn left.
And so on.

If only one pair plays at a time, use a watch to see which pair is fastest. But if there is a large space available, three or four pairs can play at the same time, one starting after another. This, of course, makes it much more difficult, as one of the ships may start to obey the wrong captain.

Students may also close their eyes if they object to being blindfolded.

46 How Did They Answer?

Purpose *To practice adverbs of manner, and answering questions in general.*

Language Required *A number of adverbs ending in -ly.*

Game One student leaves the room. The others agree on an adverb, for example, "happily." The student outside then comes back in and asks questions. The people he or she asks must answer the questions "happily," both in the way they speak and in the content of their answers.

Examples

What's the weather like today?

(Bright smile) I think it's marvelous. I love rainy days.

The student who has been outside must try to guess the adverb. He or she should ask at least six questions before making the first guess. He or she says:

I think the adverb is "happily."

Other suitable adverbs:

sadly	optimistically	laughingly	quickly
wrongly	stupidly	slowly	etc.

Comments This game will not necessarily succeed the first time because some students find it difficult to "act" the adverb. After a few times, though, the reward can be a genuine feeling for the use and meaning of adverbs.

If questions come slowly, send out a team of two instead of one student. They can ask questions in turn and confer about the guess.

47　After He Had Written His Name . . .

Purpose *To practice the simple past and pluperfect tenses.*

Language Required *Verbs for actions that can be carried out in the classroom and the necessary tenses.*

Preparation *List a number of useful verbs. These may be practiced for a short time before the game.*

Game Write a list of a dozen or so orders on the blackboard, such as:

    Stand up
    Play the piano
    Go to the door
    Jump
    Stand on your desk

One student is chosen to carry out the actions. The other students take turns giving the orders, choosing something from the list on the blackboard. They can choose items in any order. After five or six actions, the student sits down. The class must then try to remember what he or she did.

    He stood up.
    After he had stood up, he went to the blackboard.
    After he had gone to the blackboard, he wrote his name.
    After he had written his name, he opened the window.
    And so on.

Comments As the runner you might choose a student who understands the orders but who is not very good at expressing him or herself.

Writing orders on the blackboard in advance avoids two difficulties:

1. Irregular verbs that the students do not yet know.
2. Orders that cannot be carried out, for example, "Jump out of the window."

48 What's in the Square?

Purpose *To practice oral fluency in simple questions and answers. To practice "There is"/"There are."*

Language Required *The students should be well acquainted with at least one of the following constructions:*

"What's number four?"—It's a cat."

"Where's the cat?"—"It's in number four."

"What's there in square number four?"—"There's a cat in number four."

Game This game can be played with the whole class, in groups, or in pairs.

Draw a square on the blackboard, or on a piece of paper, and divide it into nine small squares. Number the squares.

1	2	3
4	5	6
7	8	9

Then draw nine objects, one in each square. For example, you might draw a cat in number one, a knife in number two, a dog in number three, a guitar in number four, and so on. The idea is to try to remember where all the objects are. If you are playing it with the whole class, go to the back of the classroom, and tell the students to look at you so they all have their backs to the blackboard, and then ask them where everything is. Several patterns are possible.

1. What's number four?
   It's a guitar.   etc.
2. Where's the guitar?
   It's in number four.   etc.
3. What's in number four?
   There's a guitar in number four.   etc.

With beginners use only one pattern during the lesson.

These last patterns can, of course, be used to practice the plural as well—in that case draw two or more objects in each square. Then ask:

1. Where are the guitars?
   They are in number four.   etc.

2. What's in number four?
    There are two guitars.   etc.

This game is also great fun when played in pairs. Each student draws a square with nine objects on a sheet of paper and then gives it to a partner who asks questions about it.

49   The "Yes" and "No" Game

Purpose *To practice general fluency and dialogue speed.*
Language Required *A general command of spoken English.*

Game The object of the game is to make your partner say "yes" or "no." For the purpose of the game, nodding or shaking your head should be counted as "yes" or "no." Anyone who says "yes" or "no" loses a life (see below).

Start off with the teacher asking the class, to show them how the game is played, and then continue working in pairs.

Example
    1: Is your name John?
    2: That's my name.
    1: Is that your only name?
    2: I'm also Peter. Do you have two names?
    1: I have only one name.
    2: Is it David?
    1: Yes, it's David.   (Number 1 loses a life.)

Give each student five "lives" and let him or her lose one each time he or she makes a mistake, that is, says "yes" or "no." In this way interest is kept up longer. The lives can be represented by chips, beans, pencils, counters, books, etc.

Comments This game must go as fast as possible, to allow very little time for thought. It is one where non-English speakers often do better than native speakers, as the latter answer automatically without pause for thought.

Alternative Instead of "yes" and "no," the forbidden words can be "I" and "my."

50 A Shouting Game

Purpose *To practice vocabulary and gain fluency.*

Language Required *This game can call on all students' reserves in spoken English, especially the names of objects in the classroom and descriptions.*

Game It is called a shouting game, although there need not be any shouting at all.

Divide the class into two teams. A player from team one goes out of the room—let's call him John—and team two chooses an object in the room. They do not need to know its English name. Let's say they choose the blackboard.

Team one must now describe the blackboard when John comes back into the room. They must not, of course, use the word "blackboard" or point to it. To start them off, help them by suggesting some phrases they could use before John comes back.

Example

It's near the teacher's desk.
It's black.
It's made of wood.
It's used every day.
We look at it often.

When John comes in, say "go" and start to time the game. Everyone in the team may now try to guide John to the object. How long is it before John guesses correctly? The shouting starts when everyone tries to guide John to it at the same time. One result is that he understands nothing at all, for everyone in the team starts talking at the same time.

There is a moral to be learned from this game, which some classes learn more quickly than others. Don't shout—if you do, you cannot be understood!

Comments Scoring: after two or three people have been out from each team, add up their time in seconds. The team with the smaller number of seconds wins. For pointing, shouting the name of the object, or not using English—add thirty seconds.

51 Quizzes

Purpose *To practice question forms and stating facts correctly.*

Language Required *The students must be so fluent that they can express themselves without thinking too much about the pattern they are using. If the quiz is based on a school textbook, it can be quite elementary.*

Preparation *Prepare a number of questions on a subject that the students should be able to talk about in English, a text in their reader, for example, or let the quiz be a test of general knowledge.*

Game A quiz can be played by teams or in pairs; the questions can be asked by the students or by the teacher.

When the teacher asks the questions
The students answer the questions orally, as members of a team, or they can write down their answers and score points individually.

The questions need not be about an English topic. You can, for example, ask questions about other subjects: history, geography, sports, movies, or a TV program that they have seen recently.

Questions should require a simple, factual answer:

What is the capital of India?
How many people live in India?
Which team won the football game here yesterday?

And so on.

Questions about passages they have read should also require factual answers.

When the students ask the questions
Get the students to prepare one, two, or three questions for homework. These should be written down so that the teacher can look through them beforehand and check that they are correct and not too difficult. A good exercise is to ask for questions based on a passage that the students have already read. In this way the passage is used as the basis for written questions and also for oral work. Students may work in pairs, or in teams.

Comments The easiest method of scoring is one point for each correct answer. Another method is to give two points for each answer, one for the facts and one for a grammatically correct answer.

52   Coffeepotting

Purpose *To practice questions and answers and promote fluency and speed.*

Language Required *A general command of spoken English.*

Game One player leaves the room. The students agree on a verb—"swim," for example. When the player comes back, he or she must try to guess the verb by asking questions that the others must answer, but they say "coffeepot" instead of the verb.

The conversation might go like this:

(1 is the player who was outside; the other numbers are the other students.)

1:   When do you coffeepot?
2:   I coffeepot in summer.
1:   Can you coffeepot in winter?
3:   Yes, you can, but most people coffeepot in the summer.
1:   Can I coffeepot?
4:   Yes, I think you can.
1:   Is it nice to coffeepot?
5:   Yes, it is.
1:   Do you coffeepot when it is raining?
6:   I usually coffeepot when the sun is shining.
1:   I think the verb is swim.

Comments This game gives the very quick students a chance to use their fluency and gives the others useful practice. When a player starts asking questions, he or she should be told to try and question all the students in the class.

This game can also be played in groups or pairs.

Alternative The class can also agree on a noun that is replaced by "coffeepot" in the questions and answers.

Example
1:   Is your coffeepot alive?
2:   No, it isn't.
1:   Can you wear your coffeepot?
3:   No, I can't.

1: Where do you use your coffeepot?

4: I use it in the street.

1: Is your coffeepot made of metal?

5: Yes, it is.

1: I think your coffeepot is a bike.

53   Making Sentences

Purpose *To practice word order.*

Language Required *The students must be fairly fluent and accurate.*

Game If the class is sitting in groups or in rows, each group or row can become a team. The object is to make a sentence, each member of the team saying one word. The sentence must contain exactly the same number of words as there are team members.

For example, if there are six members of the team:

Number one starts:	There
number two says:	are
number three says:	many
number four:	black
number five:	cats
number six:	here.

Any mistake or inability to think of a word loses a point.

Scoring: one point for each complete sentence.

A time limit, perhaps five seconds per person, is necessary.

Comments The team must not agree on a sentence beforehand. To avoid this possibility, the teacher can start off the game by giving the initial word. So, in a team of six, the sentence will have seven words.

By giving the first word, the teacher can guide the pattern of the sentence according to the standard and ability of the class.

54   The Smash-and-Grab Raid

Purpose *To practice conversation and encourage fluency, using names of stores, institutions, etc. and the activities associated with them.*

Language Required *Some knowledge of the names of stores (the grocery store, the shoe store, the florist) and some institutions (the bank, the library, the movie theater) and of things you can buy and do in them. Some previous training in conversation is essential.*

Game Draw a rough map of a small town on the board, like this:

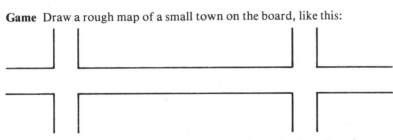

Then, helped by the class, name the streets and draw in a number of stores, offices, etc. As you fill in each one, talk a little about it.

Example

Teacher:	What's this store?
Student:	A grocery store.
Teacher:	All right. Now what can you buy here?
Student:	You can buy vegetables.
Student:	You can buy bread and milk.
Teacher:	Good, And what's this store? It's small.
Student:	A boutique.

And so on.

It is important to include a bank and a doctor's office for reasons that will soon be clear. If no student suggests them, suggest them yourself. The finished street may look like this:

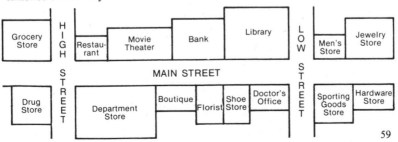

Right at the end, add a jewelry store. Then tell the following story.

At exactly 3 p.m. Saturday there was a smash-and-grab raid at the jewelry store. A car drove along Main Street, stopped outside the jewelry store, and some people jumped out. They smashed the window with a brick and grabbed as many things from the window as they could. Then they drove off. You were all in the street at that time. You were in one of the stores or in some other place. Now decide exactly where you were and what you were doing. Then you must answer some questions.

Give the class about half a minute to think about what they were doing, then ask two or three of them questions to let the others get the idea. Suitable questions are, for example:

Where were you?
What did you buy?
How much did it cost?
Why did you want to buy a . . . ?

Then, when everyone gets the idea, let students work in pairs, asking each other similar questions. Perhaps you can write a few questions on the board to help weaker students. Warn them that anyone found not having a good alibi will be needed for "further questioning by the police."

After five minutes or so, ask if anyone suspects that his or her partner does not have a good alibi. With a little prompting some suspects will soon be found. Anyone who says he or she was in the bank must be suspected because it was closed at 3 p.m. Anyone who was in the doctor's office must be suspected because it is a rare doctor who has Saturday afternoon office hours. Also, anyone is suspected if his or her answers are not appropriate to the store or location.

This game encourages intensive conversation, but can only be used once because the second time, everyone avoids the bank, the doctor's office, etc.

55   Alibi

Purpose *To practice fluent conversation using the past tenses of verbs.*
Language Required *Good command of conversational English, particularly of verbs in the past tense.*

Game Play this game only with a class that is quite good. A sense of humor helps. And at least one of the students who goes out should have a lot of imagination.

Start by telling the class about a crime that was committed the evening before. For example, a store was broken into, a building was set on fire or—if you feel particularly bloodthirsty—a teacher was murdered. The police know that this crime was committed between two definite times—say between 6 and 8 in the evening. Perhaps the store (or building, etc.) was shut at 6 and the crime discovered at 8. Two students are asked to establish an alibi for their movements between these times. They are told that they were together all the time between 6 and 8 and that everything one did, the other did, too. They can have about five minutes outside the classroom to prepare their story. When they are ready, they come in one at a time and the other students ask them detailed questions about what they did. They want to find out if the two have a good alibi—that is, if they tell exactly the same story—or if their stories are different.

While the two are outside, prepare a list of questions with the rest of the class, who play the part of the police. Write a number of questions on the blackboard. In this way students know what sort of questions to ask and, if there is a pause, the teacher can point to one of the questions and say, "Ask this question, Margaret."

Suitable questions
   Where were you at 6 o'clock?
   What were you doing?
   Where did you go after that?
   What were you wearing?
   What was your friend wearing?
   How much did the tickets cost?
   Who paid?
   Did you sit at the front or at the back   (of the bus, theater, etc.)
   Who did you speak to?
   What did you talk about?
   etc.

Once the students have asked the first "suspect" as many questions as they want to, number two comes in. The class asks him or her exactly the same questions—make them write down each question they ask, to make sure they ask each one the same questions. Very soon the class starts to realize how good or bad the story is. At the end, there is a vote: "Are they guilty or not guilty?" Those who say "Guilty" must be prepared to say why. "Peter said that the tickets cost two dollars, but Andrew said that they cost three dollars." "Peter said that they saw *Sound of Music,* but Andrew said that they saw a war movie." And so on.

Comment This game can take nearly half an hour to play.

56 The Secret Word

Purpose *To practice conversation.*

Language Required *A good command of conversational English.*

Game Two people—say, Pat and Kim—hold a conversation. Each of them tries to make the other say one particular word, given to them in advance by the teacher, but neither of them knows what the other's word is. For example, Pat may have the word "dog," so he will trv to make Kim say "dog." Kim may have the word "car," which she will try to make Pat say. The one who makes the other say the secret word is the winner.

Neither knows the word that the other is trying to make him or her say, but each will, of course, guess and try to avoid using what he or she thinks is the word.

If the other students know the two words, they enjoy listening to the conversation.

Alternative Class members can work in pairs, each one of the pair writing down a word (a noun is best) on a piece of paper before the conversation starts to use as proof when he or she wins.

57 Newspaper Reporters

Purpose *To practice questions and answers in past tenses. Writing a story as a follow-up from the game.*

Language Required *The students should be fairly advanced and have practiced some kind of story writing before.*

Game Write an outline story on the blackboard. Say it is a telegram from a news agency. A story like this usually works well:

Fire at Grand Hotel
Fire at Grand Hotel last night. Seen at 3 a.m. by *Arthur Smith* walking past. He woke *John Robinson,* porter. Phoned fire brigade. Together they woke hotel guests. *Mary Stevens,* on third floor, jumped out of window and broke leg. *June Andrews,* from same room, ran down stairs, was badly burned, now in hospital.

Four students from the class are chosen. One is Arthur Smith, one John Robinson, one Mary Stevens, and one June Andrews. The other class members are newspaper reporters who want to get the "background" to the story. They ask questions and the students at the front use their imagination in answering. For example:

Arthur Smith, why were you out at 3 in the morning?
What did you see?
John Robinson, why were you asleep?
How did you feel when they woke you up, Mary Stevens?
Why were you staying at the hotel?

The stories could later be written as a composition—a newspaper article—but this is not necessary.

Comments This game can only be used with quite advanced students who are prepared to use their imaginations. The "characters" can make up their own background—provided it fits in with the outline given—and everything each of them says can be agreed with or denied by the others.

Other Stories

A Rescue
Rosemary Stevens, on vacation, ran into the sea yesterday and saved *Peter Davidson* from drowning. Peter Davidson was swimming when he started to shout for help. Only Rosemary ran to help him. *Arthur Jones,* also on the beach, said, "I thought he was being funny."

An Accident

A car driven by *Anthony Down* hit *Mary Smith* as she was crossing the road. Her leg was broken. Mary Smith was on a pedestrian crossing. A jogger, *Susan James,* saw the accident. So did *David South,* who was looking out of a window.

A Car Thief

Margaret Davidson left her car outside her house on 52nd Street. She left her key in the car. She saw *Alfred Rose* getting into the car. She ran out and managed to pull the key from the car. She shouted for help, and *Gerald Turner* phoned the police. Margaret Davidson stayed holding the door shut until the police came.

58 Hangman

Purpose *To practice the spelling of known words.*

Language Required *The alphabet has been learned; reading and writing have started.*

Game *Hangman* is always popular, although some people seem to dislike the idea of hanging as a reminder of capital punishment. If you are one of them, draw a cat, a car, or a dog with twelve lines instead.

Think of a word and then put on the blackboard a dash for each letter of the word, e.g. (for THURSDAY):

— — — — — — — — .

The students try to guess the word, letter by letter. Every time they call out a letter that occurs in the word, it is written above the correct dash on the blackboard. Thus, the word may look like this at one point during the game:

T _ _ _ S _ A _ .

If they call out a letter that is not in the word, the teacher makes a stroke to build up the picture of the gallows (or cat, car, or dog).

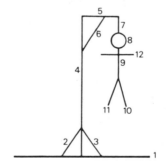

If the students complete the word before the teacher can complete the figure, they win. If the teacher completes the figure before the class can guess the word, he or she wins.

Comments Let anyone in the class call out a letter. You can, of course, ask them to speak only when it is their turn as you go round the class. But this is frustrating to anyone who has already guessed the word.

Students should only call out letters, not the complete word.

Alternatives To make the game easier, you can fill in the first or the last letter of a word yourself.

To make the game more difficult, you can also ask for the position of the letter the pupils suggest.

Is the first letter a G?
Is the fourth letter an A?

If the pupils do not know the ordinal numbers yet, they can say:

Is number four an A?

This game can also be played in groups or in pairs.

59 A Crossword Competition

Purpose *To practice the alphabet and the spelling of simple words.*

Language Required *The game can be played as soon as the students have done some reading and a little writing in English.*

Game This game can be played by two students on the blackboard or by the whole class in pairs. Each player draws a small crossword grid containing nine squares.

The players turn their backs to each other, and then take turns calling out a letter. They must both put into their crossword all the letters that are called out, both their own and their opponents'. The idea is to build as many words as possible. They are free to choose in which square to put the letter, but must not change the position of the letters once they have been written.

For example, one crossword competition might look like this after seven letters have been called out:

Number one will probably call out "A" to make the word "CAT."

Number two may then call out "O" to make "DOG."

Scoring One point for each letter in each completed word.

CAT = 3, IT = 2, and so on.

Alternative This competition can also be played in a group. Each student draws a "crossword," perhaps one with 25 squares.

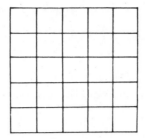

Then each member of the group calls out one letter in turn. Players must, of course, not look at each other's papers. When the crosswords are completed, score points as before, one point for each letter in each completed word.

60　Word Building

Purpose *To practice the spelling of known words.*

Language Required *Students should be used to doing written exercises.*

Game Choose a fairly long word—ENGLISHMAN, for example. The students have to make a written list of as many words as they can, using only the letters of this word. Among the words you can make from ENGLISHMAN are, for example:

　him—he—shine—meaning—miles, etc.

Three or four minutes is enough time. Let the students work on their own or in groups.

Scoring Let one student write his or her list on the blackboard. (If working in a group, others may add words he or she has not thought of.) One point for every word if it is correctly spelled, but if only one other student (or group) has that word, two points. If the student (or group) is the only one with that word, three points. The winner is the student or group with the most points.

Comment While points are being awarded, check that students know the meaning and pronunciation of the words.

61 Making Words

Purpose *To practice the spelling of known words.*

Language Required *Words must be chosen within students' vocabulary.*

Preparation *Prepare two sets of cards, each with a letter on it. Commonly used letters should have 2 or 3 cards. Alternatively, buy sets of letter cards.*

Game Divide the class into two teams. Give one letter to each member of each team. Both teams must have the same letters.

The teacher then calls out a word, for example, "Dog." The team members who have the letters D, O, and G run forward and arrange themselves as fast as possible in the correct order in front of the class, holding up their cards so that the class can read "dog." The first group to complete the word correctly gets a point for their team.

At the beginning the students usually spell the words backwards!

Some suggestions for letters and words:

Letters:	BASKETC			
Words:	basket	tea	cast	eat
	take	sat	stab	task
	bat	cats	stack	beat
	back	cakes	skate	ask
Letters:	HANDSCRE			
Words:	hands	hard	share	dance
	and	end	hare	scar
	red	can	sand	race
	head	Dane	dear	send
Letters:	ENGLANDR			
Words:	England	and	land	glad
	lend	red	grand	leg
	large	angel	grander	dare
	lane	Dane	ran	rag

Of course, not all these words are suitable for beginners and care should be taken to use words known to students. The game can be adapted to any level by selecting suitable words.

62   The Comb

Purpose *To practice spelling and to review words.*

Language Required *Words must be chosen within students' vocabulary.*

Game This is not so much a crossword puzzle as a "comb." Divide the class into two or three teams. Then write a long word on the blackboard two or three times, once for each team, spacing the letters more widely than usual.

For example:

HOLIDAY   HOLIDAY   HOLIDAY

The first member of each team runs up and fills in, downwards, a word that starts with one of the letters in "HOLIDAY." Then number two comes up, then number three, and so on. They each write one word.

For example, after number four in each team has been up, the board might look like this:

```
HOLIDAY        HOLIDAY        HOLIDAY
APO    O        E  AN  U        N IFA
PEV    U        A  N   N        L K  D
PNE             D  D   T        Y E  D
Y                              Y
```

Score one point for each letter in each correctly spelled word. Give an extra three or five points to the first team to complete their "comb" to make sure that they do not spend too much time on it. If they take too long, they often try to copy each other's "combs."

63　A Spelling Stair

Purpose *To practice spelling.*

Language Required *Words within students' vocabulary.*

Game Each team builds a "stair" on the blackboard. The first word—"dog," perhaps—has been written there in advance. Each member of the team comes forward one at a time to add a word to the stair, like this:

```
DOG
  E
  TOMORROW
        H
        E
        R
        EVERYBODY
                O
                UNCLE
```

Score one point for each letter in each word that is correctly spelled. Thus, long words are better than short ones. A spelling mistake means no points at all for that word.

Comment A weak class may be allowed to use dictionaries.

64 A Spelling Competition

Purpose *To practice recognition of words spelled orally.*

Language Required *The English alphabet should be familiar to the students. The game is best played when reading has just started.*

Game This game can be played as a team competition, or in pairs. Divide the class into two teams; give everyone in each team a number. Then ask:

What is h — o — u — s — e?

Pause: Number four.

The first number four to answer correctly—house—gets a point for his or her team.

Alternatives **(i)** One person from each team comes up to the blackboard.

Teacher: Write d — e — s — k.

The first one to write the word correctly gets a point.

(ii) Instead of writing, try drawing:

Teacher: Draw d — o — g.

Comments When the students are fairly advanced in spelling, they can play this game in pairs, practicing, for instance, the spelling of words they have had for homework.

65 Letter Cards

Purpose *To practice spelling and known words.*

Language Required *A number of words, simple or difficult, depending on the ability of the class.*

Preparation *About 60 cards, each with a letter of the alphabet on it. The most common letters, A, E, I, O, U, for example, should occur 3 times, other letters should occur twice and uncommon letters, Q, X, Z, for example, only once.*

Game A group of students draws 20 cards from the pile of cards on the teacher's desk. The cards should be in a box or a bag, so the students do not see which letters they draw. They then try to make as many English words as they can, using the letters they have drawn. They can build their words in the form of a crossword, and in this way they can use some of the letters more than once. Give a time limit, say two minutes, and then give points for each word (one point for each letter if the word is correctly spelled). Take away points for unused letters. Then another group, or team, draws 20 cards and the second round begins.

66 Heads and Tails

Purpose *To practice aural comprehension and spelling.*

Language Required *The students must be able to spell known vocabulary.*

Game This game can easily be a team competition between the two halves of the class. Give them a word to start with—"cup," for example. Team one must think of a word that starts with the last letter of "cup," that is, "p." Perhaps they say "please." Team two must then think of a word that starts with the last letter of "please," that is, "e." Perhaps they say "egg."

Team one: Go
Team two: Open
Team one: No   etc.

Anyone in the team may suggest a word, or it can be done in strict order. Give a time limit—about ten seconds is enough—and score one point for each word.

Comments This game can also be played in pairs. Advanced classes can be told to use words with four or more letters.

67 Making a Crossword on the Blackboard

Purpose *To practice the spelling of known words and to review vocabulary.*

Language Required *The students should be used to written vocabulary tests.*

Game Draw two "crosswords" on the blackboard, each containing twenty-five squares.

Team 1 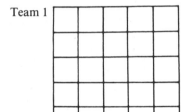   Team 2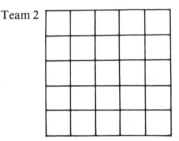

Divide the class into two teams. Give everyone in each team a number. When the teacher says "Go," number one from each team runs up to his or her team's crossword and writes a letter in one of the squares. He or she then runs back and gives number two the chalk. Number two writes one letter, gives the chalk to number three and so on until all the team members have been up to write a letter. Then number one starts again, and the game continues until all the squares are filled.

The aim is to write as many words as possible. The words can be read either across or down.

Scoring One point for each letter in a word. For example:

B	L	A	C	K
		N	A	
		D	T	O
			S	

BLACK = 5
TO = 2
AND = 3
CATS = 4

Always add five points for the team that finishes first, otherwise the teams spend a lot of time thinking about each letter, and the game can take far too long.

Comment A certain amount of talking is necessary for the team to plan which words to write.

68   Letter Bingo

Purpose *To practice the letters of the alphabet.*

Language Required *The alphabet must have been learned before the game is played.*

Preparation *Cardboard letters, stenciled bingo cards, and a hat. Prepare a set of letters on cardboard squares and a board with a space for each letter. Duplicate enough cards for each player to have several.*

Game

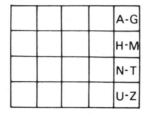

The students fill in a selection of letters—any four letters between A and G in the top row, any four letters between H and M in the second row, and so on. When everyone is ready, letters are drawn out of the hat one at a time and called clearly. To avoid misunderstanding, call "A for Apple," etc. Each letter is placed on the correct space on the teacher's board to provide a check on the winner. Students should not be able to see the board.

As each letter is called, the students check their cards, and if they have the letter, they cross it off.

The first student to get a complete line of letters which he or she has crossed off calls "Bingo"; the first to get a complete card crossed off calls "Bingo" again.

A small prize adds excitement.

69 Crossword

Purpose *To practice the meaning and spelling of words from the vocabulary students have to learn.*

Language Required *Reading and writing must have been practiced for some time.*

Game To help fix the spelling of the words, let the students make crosswords, using the given list. They may work individually or in pairs and should use squared paper. Paper stenciled with 1cm squares is best. Thus, the following list:

window-cleaner	shed	garden	wonder
wait	ladder	street	against
woman	carry	watch	climb

might result in this crossword:

```
                                                        ③
          ②                                              C
      ① C  L  I  M  B              ④                      A
  ⑤       A     ⑦                  G                      R
  ⑥ W  I  N  D  O  W  -  C  L  E  A  N  E  R              R
    A     D     O                 R                      Y
    T     E     M        ⑧        D
    C     R     A     ⑨ S  T  R  E  E  T
    H           N        H        N
                ⑩        E
             ⑪ W  O  N  D  E  R
                A
      ⑫ A  G  A  I  N  S  T
                T
```

When the students have gotten as many words as they can into the crossword, they number the words and write the translation beside the crossword.

The winner is the student with the most words correctly written in a crossword.

70   Picture and Word Lotto

Purpose *To practice the reading of single nouns.*

Language Required *The game is most useful when the students have been practicing reading for a couple of months.*

Preparation *Draw or cut from magazines pictures of simple objects. The students should know all their names. Each name should be written on a separate card. There should be sufficient sets of these word-cards for each student to have up to ten different ones.*

Game The teacher has the pictures which he or she can either hold up or show on an overhead projector. The students have the word-cards.

As a picture is shown, the student with the corresponding word-card holds it up and calls out the word. If the word is pronounced correctly, that word-card is put aside and counts one point. If several students show the correct card, the first one wins the point. If you wish, the same picture may be shown again later in the game to give the others a chance.

Comment Luck as well as skill is needed to win the game, so the less able students have a chance, too.

71   The Classroom in Letters

Purpose *To review the English alphabet and the names of things in the classroom.*

Language Required *Nouns (the names of things in the classroom) and the alphabet.*

Game Students work in groups of not more than five. Each group tries to write down an "alphabet'" of things in the classroom. They begin with "A" and go on to "B," "C," etc. Omit difficult letters like "Q," "X," and "Z."

Example
   atlas
   blackboard
   curtains
   desk

Score one point for each correct word. If the students write more than one word for each letter, and you have suggested that they do this, score one point for the first word and half a point for each of the others.

Comment If you want to stress spelling, score one point for an intelligible word and an extra point for the correct spelling.

72   A Word Snake

Purpose *To practice spelling.*

Language Required *The students must have a general vocabulary of at least three or four hundred words and be able to spell these words.*

Game This game is similar to make a crossword, but it is easier to adjust to different rules and levels of teaching.

Each student needs several snakes like that in the diagram.

The teacher must determine the number of squares. If the students prepare the "snake," check that they all have the same number of squares.

The students fill the snake with properly spelled words so that there are no empty squares and no letters outside the snake. The competition is to see how many can fill the snake with correctly spelled words within a limited time, for instance, three or four minutes. Played this way, the game can be used once or twice at an early stage. It is also possible to play the game in pairs or in groups of three or four, the pairs or groups competing with each other.

Give points for each correctly spelled word, one point for each letter, and take off points for spelling mistakes.

Alternatives (i) Play the game as above, but allow only words from a certain subject—the weather, sports, house, garden, geography, or clothes.

(ii) Allow only nouns or adjectives or verbs.

(iii) Divide the class up into groups of five or six students. The students fill in one word each, passing the snake round in the group. Two or three students may have to write more than one word.

The group that completes its snake first is the winner.

(iv) Play the game in pairs. The two pupils take turns filling in a word in the snake. The one who succeeds in finishing the snake is the winner. Each pair needs at least three snakes.

(v) More difficult. Each word must start with the last letter of the previous word, thus, using this letter twice. If the snake is finished with the same letter as the first letter of the first word, give an extra point. Such a snake could look like this:

(vi) More difficult. The snake must contain a full sentence. Play in pairs, each player contributing alternate words. The first pair to finish correctly wins.

73   Let's Open a Store

Purpose *To practice the names of articles and commodities that can be bought in different stores.*

Language Required *The names of stores and items that can be bought in them.*

Preparation *Cards with the names of stores and articles that can be bought there.*

Game Prepare a number of pieces of paper, each containing the name of a store, e.g., Supermarket, Hardware Store, Butcher, Baker, Florist. Prepare as many cards as possible, at least six for each shop. Each has on it one item that can be bought in the shop, e.g.

Supermarket	Hardware Store	Bakery	Butcher	Florist
tea	hammer	white bread	beef	roses
sugar	nails	a cake	lamb	flowers
carrots	ruler	brown bread	sausages	daffodils
butter	saw	rolls	mutton	tulips
apples	wrench	pastries	pork	carnations
lettuce	screwdriver	cookies	steak	irises
etc.	etc.	etc.	etc.	etc.

Divide the class into teams. Each team is given a card with the name of a store on it. The smaller cards are hidden around the room. The students search for the correct items for their team's store. There should be a time limit on the search. Points are awarded for each correct item, and taken off for cards taken to the wrong store. If it is preferred, the cards need not be hidden. Students select the ones they need.

Comments As a follow-up to this game, groups can use the cards as the basis of a situational conversation involving shopping. After some time the students might manage without the cards and do their "shopping" on the basis of what they *want* to buy.

A "shopping conversation" could be written on the blackboard to guide the students. For example:

1:   Yes, sir/Yes, ma'am?
2:   A box of tea, please.
1:   Here you are. Anything else?
2:   A pound of sugar, please.

1: Anything else?
2: No, thank you. How much is that?
1: Two dollars, please. Thank you. Goodby.
2: Goodby.

Alternatives **(i)** Show the class a number of pictures and ask them, for example, "Where did I buy this pair of shoes?" They can either say the answer aloud or write it: "You bought it at a shoe store."

(ii) Ask the questions without showing the pictures.

74 Numbered Commands

Purpose *To practice written instructions.*

Language Required *A fairly good knowledge of nouns, the names of things in the classroom, some common verbs, and prepositions of place.*

Preparation *Prepare a set of number cards.*

Game Write a number of commands on the blackboard. For example:

1. Sit on the teacher's desk.
2. Write your name on the blackboard.
3. Open the door.
4. Put your pencil on the floor
5. Sit on the teacher's chair facing backwards.
6. Tell me the time.
   And so on.

Divide the class into two or three teams, and then number the members of each team. There must be many more commands on the blackboard than there are members of each team.

The teacher puts the cardboard numbers into a hat, shakes them, and says, for example, "Number one." He or she then pulls out a number and shows it to the class. The number ones find the corresponding command on the blackboard and hurry to obey it. The student who is first to obey the correct command gets one point for his or her team.

The game continues until all the students have had a turn. The winning team is the one with the highest number of points.

Alternative Write commands on separate pieces of paper and put the pieces of paper in a box. One student draws a command out of the box and then silently carried out that command. The others try to guess *exactly* what is written on the paper. They can guess aloud or in writing. This may be played with two teams and points awarded.

75   You Are a Cowboy

Purpose *To practice the names of occupations and animals.*
Language Required *Enough English to be able to identify a number of occupations and animals.*

Game Divide the class into two teams. Give each person in each team a number. When the two students hear their number called, they run out to the teacher who either whispers or writes down a role for them, for example:

You are a cowboy.

The two run back to their respective teams and mime a cowboy. When the team can guess the right answer, one writes it down, and a runner takes it to the teacher.

He (she) is a cowboy.

The first team with the correct answer gets two points, and the second team gets one point if their answer is also correct.

Call numbers in any order until everyone has had a turn.

Comment They need not necessarily write the answer; they could, of course, call it out.

Some suggestions

You are:

a pilot	a teacher	a boxer
a police officer	a taxi driver	a singer
a dentist	a tennis player	a seaman
a doctor	a football player	a store clerk

Instead of jobs you can use the names of animals. You are:

a tiger	a fish	a snake
a cat	a duck	a pig
a dog	a cow	a pig
an elephant	a horse	a sheep

76 Words for a Subject

Purpose *To practice known vocabulary and learn new words relating to a chosen subject.*

Language Required *The students should have a working knowledge of about 700 words, and they should be able to look words up in a dictionary or word list.*

Game Work in groups of three to five students. Each group should have access to a dictionary or word list. Choose—together with the class—a subject that interests as many as possible or one that relates to material recently read.

Perhaps the subject chosen is "Football." The different groups try to find as many words as possible to do with football.

Examples

ball	touchdown	huddle	bowl game
player	punt	flag	halftime
goal	referee	pass	field goal
quarterback	whistle	kick	coach

The words are awarded points, either one point for each correct word, or one point for nouns and two points for verbs.

Possible subjects

Kitchen, Bedroom	The Classroom	Sports	Cars
Buildings	The Farm	Clothes	The Weather
The Garden	Music	Food	Hobbies

Comments The words chosen for fairly simple subjects may turn out to be quite advanced! Don't forget to help the class with the pronunciation of any new words.

77 Odd Man Out

Purpose *To recognize common factors in a group of words and pick irrelevant words.*

Language Required *Whatever stage the class's vocabulary has reached. Each group of five words contains one "odd man out"—a word which does not fit.*

Preparation *Lists of words within the class's vocabulary.*

Game The teacher writes the lists on the blackboard. The students should be able to pick out the irrelevant word and say why it is the "odd man out."

Example

hat	scarf	cat	coat	tie

In this list, cat is an animal and the other words are clothes. Answers may be written or oral.

Other groups of words

red	blue	black	small	yellow

(colors + size)

tree	house	tent	cottage	apartment

(can live in + can't live in)

car	bike	motorcycle	truck	bus

(has a motor + no motor)

sing	talk	listen	chat	shout

(with mouth + with ears)

bird	airplane	fly	helicopter	spider

(can fly + can't fly)

The groups of words can be made harder or easier, depending on the ability of the class.

Comment Classes enjoy making the lists of words themselves and asking each other. This is very good practice.

78 Jumbled Words

Purpose *To practice spelling.*

Language Required *Nouns relevant to the subject chosen.*

Preparation *The teacher must prepare a number of groups of jumbled words, each group relating to a theme.*

Game The students work individually or in teams to identify the words within a given time, say one minute for each group of words. The winner is the one with the most words correct.

Examples

This is what I ate for breakfast:

SOTAT	CRONSLAFEK
TRUBET	KLIM
AJM	GARUS

(Toast, butter, jam, cornflakes, milk, sugar)

In the classroom you can see:

LOBBARCKAD	SOKOB
KLACH	ECRATHE
OROD	SDEDNSUTT

(Blackboard, chalk, door, books, teacher, students)

In a city, you can find:

TROSES	TOSATIN
SVIMOE	GNIRKAP OTL
YCTI LAHL	RABILYR

(Stores, movies, city hall, station, parking lot, library)

Alternative Let each team work out a list of jumbled words which the other teams can try to solve. Each group of words should have a common theme until the class is very skilled, when single, difficult words may be used. This is a good way to encourage students to learn the new words in a text.

79 Out-of-Order Sentences

Purpose *To practice and evaluate reading comprehension.*

Language Required *The students should be quite used to reading.*

Preparation *Take a passage the students know well, and change the order of the sentences. Arrange them in a list. Make stenciled copies of the list.*

Game Give each student a copy of the list of jumbled sentences. They must rearrange the sentences to make a coherent narrative. To make the sentences shorter and the task not quite so easy, the teacher may rephrase the story a little before jumbling the sentences.

Here is an example:

Bad luck again.
John went out of the booth, wondering what to do.
He went in and searched his pockets for a dime.
He found one in Baker Street.
Ring-ring. Ring-ring.
He hung up and then tried again.
No answer.
He looked around for a phone booth.
He found one, put it in the slot, and dialed the number.
John wanted to call his friend Martin.

John wanted to call his friend Martin. He looked around for a phone booth. He found one in Baker Street. He went in and searched his pockets for a dime. He found one, put it in the slot, and dialed the number. Ring-ring. Ring-ring. No answer. He hung up and then tried again. Bad luck again. John went out of the booth, wondering what to do.

Alternatives (i) Unknown texts may be used to see if the students can put them together in a logical order.

(ii) After some practice, the students can jumble sentences themselves and give them to each other to solve.

80   Treasure Hunt

Purpose *To practice obeying written orders.*

Language Required *Names for things in the classroom and prepositions of place.*

Space *The game can be played in a classroom, but a gym or a playground is better.*

Preparation *The teacher must prepare the clues and hide them.*

Game A number of clues are hidden around the room, each one leading to the next, until the final clue leads to the "treasure," a small prize. The students go round the "course" in pairs.

The clues can be simple, for example:

Look under the clock.
Look behind the map of the United States.
The next clue is on the wall to the left of the door in the classroom.

Write a letter, or a word, on the back of each clue. These letters, or words, should lead to the final treasure. If a number of pairs are going around the course at the same time, get them to copy the clues (or the "key words") as they go around, to avoid their watching where others go and, thus, taking a short cut to the treasure. The winners are those who complete the course first.

Alternatives (i) The game can be made more difficult by harder clues, perhaps in the form of riddles. For example:

I have a face but no head. Look behind me (the clock)
I am black (green) but become white when you write (the blackboard)

(ii) Use jumbled words:

Look in a REWARD in a KEDS. The clue can be hidden in any drawer, in any desk. You need not define exactly where to look.
Look under a RAICH. (Don't say which chair.)

(iii) Use indirect clues:

Look in a dark place. (This could mean a drawer, a cupboard, or anywhere else you might like to try.)

81　What Page?

Purpose *To use books and papers for information.*

Language Required *The contents of an English book previously studied by the class.*

Game The teacher reads out a sentence from the book. The sentence should be read out only once or twice, but it should be typical of a passage in the book. The students each have a copy of the book and try to find the page on which the sentence occurs. They write down the page number and perhaps even the line number, if it is marked in the book. Do not allow unlimited time—about 1 minute is long enough, unless the book is very long.

The winner is the student with the greatest number of correct page numbers.

This competition can be an amusing way of starting review of a textbook at the end of the school year. With Alternative (i) it provides a useful preparation for reading for information.

Alternatives (i) Each student, or group of students, gets a copy of the same newspaper or magazine. Pick out a number of lines from different articles and ask them to find the lines in the paper. The lines should contain a clue to the right page.

For example

goal from the thirty-yard line

probably comes from the sports page, while

the mayor said in a speech yesterday

probably comes from the front page or the political news.

This alternative can be made easier by giving the students a longer passage to find.

(ii) Let the students practice looking for information in a newspaper or magazine, not known to them before. They need to be fairly advanced in English and to be able to understand the contents of newspaper articles in general terms (Level C). They try to answer, orally or in writing, a number of questions from the teacher. The first question can be quite simple, for example:

On what page is there a picture of the President?

Where are the football scores?

How much does the paper cost?

More difficult questions are, for example:

On what page can you read about a fashion show?
What is the name of the President's son?
How many touchdowns did (name of team) make?
Where did the traffic accident happen?
What will the weather be like tomorrow?

The competition can be either to find the answers first or to get the most correct answers.

82 When Are You Going to Arrive?

Purpose *To practice reading and understanding a timetable and words for journeys.*

Language Required *Enough English to be able to read a timetable, including the notes.*

Preparation *A train, bus, or plane timetable from an English-speaking country. The teacher must prepare the questions in advance. Sometimes the students need explanations of words found in a timetable.*

Game If each student or group of students has a copy of the same timetable, the teacher can read out the questions. If not, the questions should be written—on small pieces of paper—and attached to different pages or different timetables, which are then passed between the groups—or from person to person.

The questions should be easy to answer by studying the timetables. For example:

What time does the first plane leave New York for Chicago on a Sunday morning?
When does it arrive in Chicago?
Is there a connection to Los Angeles?
The concert finishes in Detroit at 11:00 p.m. It takes at least 20 minutes to get to the bus station. When does the last bus leave for Ann Arbor?
What time does it arrive in Ann Arbor? Is there a train on Saturday from Phoenix to New Orleans?

The students should write their answers down and then pass the timetable page with the written questions to the next group or student.

If a complete timetable is used, questions about fares, etc. can also be asked, based on information to be found in the front. For example:

Does a child of 12 pay half price?
How much luggage can you take free?
etc.

83 Making a Sentence

Purpose *To practice fluency.*

Language Required *The students should be used to writing English.*

Game Choose a fairly long word. Then the students—or groups of students—try to make a sentence in which each word starts with one letter of the word, used in the correct order.

Examples

ARMCHAIR can become
A Russian man came home and immediately rang.
COMPETITION can become
Charles once met Polly early Tuesday in town instead of Nancy.

The best sentence may be read to the whole class.

84   Last Word Chain

Purpose *To practice fluency in writing correct sentences.*

Language Required *The students should have written sentences on their own before.*

Game This game can be played orally, but the written form is much easier. It should be played in groups of five or six. Each member of the group writes a short sentence. Then the sentences are passed on to the person sitting on the left. Everyone now writes a new sentence beginning with the last word of the first sentence. Thus, in a group of six each member writes six different sentences. For example:

Today is Friday.
Friday is a long day at school.
School takes too much time.
Time is money.
Money is good to have.
Have you finished your sentence yet?

Scoring: Five points for each correct sentence.

Comments Perhaps you should not pay too much attention to spelling in this game, since fluency is more important. It is possible, however, to take away one point for a spelling mistake but to leave the remaining points if the sentence is otherwise correct.

Alternative The game is much more difficult if the sentences have to fit together to make a complete context.

85   Homemade Quizzes

Purpose *To practice fluency using different kinds of questions in different tenses.*

Language Required *The students must have a working knowledge of basic grammatical patterns.*

Game Divide the class into four equal groups. Each group works for some time on the preparation of ten questions, which they write on a piece of paper. The questions should all be on a certain subject agreed upon in advance. You had better check the questions so that they are not too difficult.

When all the questions have been prepared, the four teams start a competition and play a full round:

Team 1 v. Team 2, Team 3 v. Team 4.

Team 1 v. Team 3, Team 2 v. Team 4.

Team 1 v. Team 4, Team 2 v. Team 3.

Each team asks the other teams their questions, reading from their lists. The team scoring most correct answers wins.

If a team is caught not knowing the correct answer to their own questions, they lose two points.

Suggested subjects:

Sports
Geography
Films
Pop music
Famous persons   etc.

Comment A book or part of a book that the class has just read makes a good subject for questions. This is a painless form of review.

86   Split Sentences

Purpose *To practice comprehension and knowledge of structures.*

Language Required *Fairly good command of reading and writing.*

Preparation *Choose a passage from a textbook. Split the sentences and arrange the parts in any order.*

Game When you first play this game, choose a passage that the class has read. Later, you can choose a passage they do not know.

Example

> Sam hadn't eaten anything for two days. He got to a river and decided to try fishing. He made a hook out of two twigs. He found a piece of string in his pocket. He dug two worms out of a rotten log. He sat down and dropped his line into the water. But when a fish took the worm the hook broke.

Now split up the sentence, like this, for example:

Sam hadn't eaten anything	out of two twigs.
He got to a river and	for two days.
He made a hook	in his pocket.
He found a piece of string	out of a rotten log.
He dug two worms	the hook broke.
He sat down and	decided to try fishing.
But when a fish took the worm	dropped his line into the water

Students have to join the sentences correctly. The first to do so is the winner. This game demands an understanding of meaning and a knowledge of structures.

Alternatives (i) After some examples from the teacher, the students can split the sentences themselves and swap sets of sentence pairs like the ones above.

(ii) Odd sentences or imperative phrases could be used in the same way. Try, for example, the school rules.

Here are some examples taken from advertisements and signs of different kinds:

Do not walk	the elephants.
Shut	in our cakes.
No talking	on the grass.
Do not feed	at 8 o'clock.
Do not smoke	for the operator.
No left turn	after lights out.
This store opens	in the dining room.

We use butter
Dial O

between 4-6 p.m.
this door.

87   Questions and Answers

Purpose *To .practice reading comprehension and the writing of questions and answers.*
Language Required *General practice in reading and writing English.*

Game Divide the class into two teams, a Question team and an Answer team. The members of the Question team write questions on the homework. The members of the Answer team write answers to questions they *think* they will get. A number of questions and answers, perhaps 20, should be decided on beforehand.

The students in the Question team take turns reading a question, and the members of the Answer team try to find the correct answer among those they have written. If there is no really correct answer, they must take the one that they think is best. That way, however, they lose one answer that they might use later on. Each answer may be used once only.

Score one point for the Answer team if they have the correct answer, one point for the Question team if the correct answer cannot be found.

To avoid cheating and unnecessary discussions, the teacher should collect the questions and answers after they have been used.

Alternative If the class needs practice in using interrogatives, it is a good idea to ask questions beginning with "What" in the first round, questions beginning with "When" in the second round, and then with "Where," "Why," and "How." This way you also give the Answer team a chance to vary their sentence building.

88 Interviews

Purpose *To practice fluency in a question-and-answer situation.*

Language Required *Enough English to be able to carry on a reasonably fluent conversation within the limits of their vocabulary and knowledge of grammatical structures.*

Preparation *Students should each choose a well-known historical person and find out a certain amount about him or her before the game.*

Game A group of three or four students work together. One of them takes the part of a well-known person, the others interview him or her. Later they can exchange roles.

They can ask about the person's private life, family, and the work he or she has done; also why he or she did certain things, etc.

The rest of the class can retell what they have heard in the interview.

Alternatives (i) The whole class can represent a press conference where an unlimited number of reporters can ask questions.

(ii) The group or class can think up an imaginary situation as the reason for the interview. For example:

The President after a burglary at the White House.
A well-known movie star who has just become a senator.

(iii) Choose a character from a book that the pupils have read and interview him or her.

89   I Pass the Scissors Crossed

Language Required *Knowledge of what the words "crossed" and "uncrossed" mean.*

Game A number of students sit in a circle. The teacher, or a student who knows the secret, is the leader. The leader starts the game by passing a pair of scissors to the person on the right, saying at the same time, "I pass the scissors uncrossed" or "I pass the scissors crossed." The other students try to guess what is meant by "crossed" and "uncrossed," and pass the scissors around the circle each saying either "I pass the scissors crossed" or "I pass the scissors uncrossed." The leader tells them if they are right or wrong.

Many ways are tried: the scissors are open or closed, but the students soon find that this does not necessarily work. They try holding them with their hands above or below the scissors, or using their left or their right hands. None of these variations are correct. By watching the leader do it, some realize the secret.

"Crossed" or "uncrossed" refers to the way the speaker has his or her legs, so if you say "I pass the scissors crossed," your legs must be crossed. It does not matter how you hold the scissors.

This can be very frustrating for students who think they know the secret and then find they are wrong.

Comment This game should not be played with very young students. If it is, safety scissors should be used.

90   Black Magic

Language Required *The students need to know the names of a few things in the classroom and the phrases, "Is it this?", "No, it isn't," and "Yes, it is."*

Preparation *One or more of the students must be told the secret before the game.*

Game A student who knows the secret leaves the room; the game is more "magical" if the others do not know there is a secret and think the teacher has chosen the student by chance.

The rest choose a certain object in the classroom, and, when the student returns, the teacher asks, "Is it this?", pointing to an object in the room. The student answers, "No, it isn't," and the teacher then points to another object and asks, "Is it this?" again. The student again answers "No" and the question is repeated. The student answers "No" all the time until asked about the correct object, when, to everyone's surprise, he answers, "Yes, it is."

The secret is simple. The correct object is the one immediately after a black object, so as soon as the teacher points to anything black, the student knows that the next object is the correct one.

You can, of course, vary the color to make it more difficult for the rest of the class to guess.

Alternative You can use a number code—for example, the correct object is the sixth you ask, etc. As this is quite easy to guess, you can use a telephone number that you both know—4946, for example. Thus, the first correct object would be the fourth object pointed at; the second time you did the trick, the ninth, etc..

91 Spinning the Plate

Space *A gym or playground is better than a classroom.*

Equipment *A tin plate.*

Language Required *Numbers.*

Game A number of students sit on the floor in a circle. Give each one a number. (Don't necessarily begin with number one. If you want to practice higher numbers, start with number 61, for example.) In the middle of the circle is a tin plate (it won't break). One student goes to the center and spins the plate on its edge, at the same time calling out a number, before running back to place. The student with that number must run to the middle and catch the plate before it falls over. If successful, then he or she spins the plate and calls another number. If, on the other hand, the plate falls over, he or she is out, or else loses a "life," depending on the rules made up.

Comment If students are "out," the one who spins the plate must not call their number. If or she does so by mistake, he or she will be out, as no one will come to catch the plate.

92   Shouting a Line

Language Required *Enough English to be able to recognize words and sentences under difficult circumstances.*

Game Divide the class into two teams. One team then chooses a well-known quotation. It could be the first line of a song that everyone knows, a sentence that will be easily recognized, or a proverb if the class knows any. Then divide the words up among the members of the team. For example, if the team chooses, "My Bonnie lies over the ocean," number one would have "My," number two "Bonnie," number three "lies," and so on. If there are more members of the team than there are words in the sentence, start again with "My," "Bonnie," "lies," etc. until everyone has a word.

Then the teacher says "Now" and everyone in the team, at the same time, shouts out his or her word. The other team must try to guess the sentence that is being shouted. They get a point if they do. Then they choose a sentence. And so on.

Comment A short sentence, especially one with one or two easily discernible words ("Bonnie" and "ocean" in the example above) works more easily than a longer sentence.

A *very* noisy game!

93 Consequences

Language Required *Some practice in reading and writing.*

Game This is a writing game, best played in a small group, perhaps to cheer the students up after hard work.

Everyone has paper and pencil. They each write a story, but after writing the first line, they fold the paper over so that what they have written cannot be seen, and pass the paper on to the next person.

The teacher says, "His name was . . . " Everyone writes a *man's name* at the top of the paper, folds down the paper and passes it on. The teacher says, "He met . . . " Everyone writes a *woman's name,* folds down the paper and passes it on. "They met at . . . " Everyone writes the *name of the place* where they met, folds down the paper and passes it on. "He said to her . . . " Everyone writes *what he said,* folds down the paper and passes it on. "She said to him . . . " Everyone writes *what she said,* folds down the paper and passes it on. "And then they both . . . " Everyone writes *what they did* and folds down the paper.

The papers are then collected, mixed, and everyone gets a paper to unfold. Everyone then reads the story he has got aloud. The story, a product from six different writers, should be illogical and funny. One's own name occurs often (so does the principal's!) and they both invariably say "I love you."

Read the papers aloud in this way: (Name) met (name) at (place). He said, (" . . . "). She said, (" . . . "). And then they (. . .).

94 What Would Your Friend Choose?

Language Required *Familiarity with question-and-answer exercises and games.*

Preparation *A number of questions within the class's vocabulary.*

Game The students work in pairs. The pairs should, if possible, be friends, or know each other well. For adult students, the ideal pair is husband and wife.

One member of a pair goes out. The other member then answers a number of questions about the person who is out of the room, trying to guess correctly what he or she would choose. Some can be multiple-choice questions, for example:

What would he (she) choose for his (her) birthday?
  a dog?
  a bicycle?
  a new coat?
Which lesson does he (she) like best?
  English?
  Mathematics?
  Woodwork?

Other questions need have no answers suggested:

What is his (her) favorite color?
What is his (her) favorite food?
What kind of music does he (she) like best?

After the first member of the pair has tried to answer the questions, the other one comes in and gives his own answers. A correct choice by number one gives the pair one point. The team with the most points wins.

Some other questions that can have answers of a multiple-choice type:

What would he (she) choose for lunch?
What would he (she) spend $5.00 on?
What would he do if he saw the school was on fire?
Where would he (she) like to go on vacation?
What job would he (she) choose?
What would he (she) like to do in the evening?

95 The Train from New York to Philadelphia

Space *A hall or a playground is better than a classroom.*

Equipment *A scarf to blindfold one student (optional).*

Language Required *The students should know and be able to pronounce the names of some well-known towns and cities and to understand expressions like "The train is now going from New York to
Philadelphia." "All change."*

Game All the players except one sit in a circle. The remaining player stands in the middle of the circle, blindfolded or with eyes closed. All the
seated players are now given the name of a well-known town or city.
Before the game starts, each pupil in the circle calls out the name of his or
her town or city so that the blindfolded player has a chance to hear where
they are situated. (You had better make a note of the towns yourself, or let
each player hold a piece of paper with the town written on it, since it is
very easy to forget the order.)

You now choose two towns situated opposite each other and call out,
for instance:

The train is now going from New York to Philadelphia.

Immediately the two students get up and quietly change places, crossing
the circle. As they are doing so, the blindfolded student tries to catch one
of them.

If, after a few changes, nobody has been caught, you call out:

All change.

Each player in the circle changes places with a player sitting opposite. In
the chaos that is certain to arise in the middle of the circle, somebody is
bound to be caught. Anyone caught is blindfolded and takes the place in
the middle of the circle, and the player who was there before becomes a
town, taking the paper with the name on it.

96 Charades

Game The class is divided into teams and each team chooses a word of two or more syllables. Each syllable must itself be a word. At this level, compound nouns are best.

Examples

    arm + chair
    after + noon
    any + thing
    bath + room
    down + stairs
    foot + ball   etc

The team choosing "football" will prepare three short scenes—one containing the world "foot," one "ball," and the third "football." The rest of the class try to guess the word.

A useful rule is that the word must be said at least twice during the scene, but the scene need not necessarily center around the word.

The teacher must decide whether the students' native language should be prohibited during the preparation of the charade or not.

Comment Charades need lots of practice, but can be very rewarding. Most classes enjoy them very much.

97 Clue

Language Required *Fluency in spoken English.*

Preparation *A number of slips of paper, one for each player. "Criminal" is written on one, "Detective" on another. All the other slips are blank.*

Game Each person draws one of the slips of paper. The person who gets the slip with the word "criminal" on it is, of course, the criminal. All students are asked to move anywhere they like in the room, but upon hearing the word *STOP* must stand still and cover their eyes completely. The "criminal" will quietly go and tap someone on the shoulder; this person now becomes the "victim." The teacher gives the criminal time to return to a position in the room and then instructs students to uncover their eyes. The victim identifies himself or herself and is seated at the front of the room. The detective will likewise identify himself and will then try to find out who the criminal is by asking questions. The rule is that everyone *must* tell the truth except the criminal, who may lie as much as he or she likes in order not to be found out. The victim cannot be questioned.

The detective can ask questions such as, "Where were you when you stopped?" "Who was on your left (right)?" "Did you hear anyone move?" "Did you open your eyes?"

When the detective knows who the criminal is, he or she must make a direct accusation and say, "I think you are the criminal." If the accusation is correct, the criminal must now tell the truth and confess. (If the detective asks a question, "Are you the criminal?" the criminal can lie and say "No." If the detective is correct, he wins; if he is wrong, the criminal wins.)

Comments This game can be played several times running. It is better in a small group than in a complete class.

98   Explain Yourself

Language Required *Fluency in spoken English.*

Game A student is given a sentence. He or she has a few minutes to think, and then must tell the rest of the class a story that ends with the sentence that he or she was given. One such sentence might be:

"And there was I, in a bathing suit, sitting on a bull, riding through the center of the town."

The rest of the class may know the final sentence in advance, or can hear the whole story up to the final sentence and then try to guess what it is.

Other sentences

I felt very silly when the principal looked under the table and found me sitting there, eating an ice cream cone.

So I jumped up and rang the bell.

I was embarrassed when the crowds started to cheer me as I walked across the main street.

There I was, high up in the swaying tree, just reaching for the silly cat, when she jumped down and ran away as fast as she could.

I had to start all over again.

But when I got out of the train, there was no one at the station to meet me.

And I never answered the telephone again.

Index of Purposes: What You Can Practice

Aim	Game Number		
	Level A	Level B	Level C
Adjectives, colors	6, 22	6, 9, 22	9
general	2, 6	6, 9, 25a, 26	9
of mood	3	26	
of quality		26, 39	
Adverbs, of direction		10, 44, 45	10, 44, 45
of manner			46
Alphabet, letters of the	20, 59, 71	59, 64, 68, 71	
Articles		29	29
Commands, oral	1, 3, 6	6, 10, 41, 44 45	10, 41, 44, 45,
written	80	74, 80	
Conversational phrases	21	21, 52, 73	52, 54, 55, 56, 57
Descriptions, animals and things	24a	9, 24a, 50	9, 50
people		9	9
Directions		10, 44	10, 44
Do-Did		36, 37, 39	
Do you have, Does he have		30, 31	
Does		35, 36a	
Fluency, oral	48	36, 42, 48, 49, 50, 52, 94	42, 47, 49, 50 52, 53, 54, 55 56, 88, 94, 96, 97, 98
written		79, 83, 84, 85 86, 93	57, 79, 83, 84 85, 86, 87, 88
Greetings	21	21	
Interrogatives	32, 48	33, 36, 39, 44 48	44, 47, 55, 87a
Irregular verbs		37, 38, 40, 41	40, 41, 47
Listening comprehension	1-5, 6-8	4, 5, 6-10, 29, 66, 81, 92	7-10, 29, 81
Nouns	6, 23, 24, 30 31	6, 9, 23, 24 25, 33, 35, 74	9
animals	5	5, 74	
the body	1		
things in the classroom	2, 5, 22, 23, 71 90	5, 22, 23, 71 74, 80, 90	
clothes	2, 5, 22	5, 22	
things in a house		43, 44	43, 44
professions		39, 74	

Aim	Game Number		
	Level A	Level B	Level C
school material	2, 24, 30, 31	24, 33	
stores		73	54
subject areas	5	5, 76, 78, 82	76, 78, 82
things to buy		25, 29, 73	29, 54
towns (names of)		25, 95	95
things in a town		10	10, 54
Numbers, cardinal	2, 15-18, 91	17-19, 91	
Polite phrases	1, 21	21	
Position, adverbs & prepositions	4, 6, 24a	4, 6, 9, 24a 34, 43, 44, 45 74, 80	9, 43, 44, 45
Prepositions, of direction	1	10, 44, 45	10, 44, 45
of place	4, 6, 24a	4, 6, 9, 10 24a, 34, 43 44, 74, 80	9, 10, 43, 44
Pronunciation	12	12, 14, 25, 28 33	14, 28
distinctness	12	12, 14	14
rhyming		13	
rhythm & stress	12	12, 14	14
vowels & diphthongs	11		
Questions,	8, 30, 31, 32, 48	8, 34, 39, 48 51, 52, 85	8, 51, 52, 85, 87, 88
Are you?	32a	39, 43	43
Do you?		39, 52	52
Do you have?—Does he have	30, 31	40	40
Is it?	23	23, 34	
Is/Are there?		33	
Reading comprehension	70	70, 79, 80, 81 82, 86	79, 81, 82, 86 87
Sentence building	31	38, 51, 83, 84 86	46, 51, 53, 83 84, 86
Some		29	29
Spelling	58-60, 69	59-68, 69, 72 76	60, 69, 76
Tenses, the conditional		42	42
the past		29, 35a, 37 38, 41	29, 41, 47, 55, 56
the perfect		38, 40	40
the pluperfect		38	47
the present cont.	32		
the present sing. (-s)		35, 38	
There is/are	48	33, 48	
Third person sing. (-s)		35, 38	
Verbs,	6, 32	6, 27, 36, 38 41, 74	27, 41, 55
of action (See Tenses)	1, 3, 6	6, 27, 38, 40, 41, 42, 52	27, 40, 41, 42, 47, 52

Aim	Game Number		
	Level A	Level B	Level C
Vocabulary, general	8, 58, 60, 69 70	8, 28, 35, 37 39, 50, 60, 61 62, 63, 64, 65 66, 67, 69, 70 72, 76, 77, 78, 82	8, 28, 50, 60 69, 76, 77, 78 82
Word order			53

a after game number indicates Alternative.

NTC ESL/EFL TEXTS AND MATERIAL
Junior High—Adult Education

Computer Software
Amigo
Basic Vocabulary Builder on Computer

Language and Culture Readers
Beginner's English Reader
Advanced Beginner's English Reader
Cultural Encounters in the U.S.A.
Passport to America Series
  California Discovery
  Adventures in the Southwest
  The Coast-to-Coast Mystery
  The New York Connection
Discover America Series
  California, Chicago, Florida, Hawaii,
  New England, New York, Texas,
  Washington, D.C.
Looking at America Series
  Looking at American Signs, Looking at
  American Food, Looking at American
  Recreation, Looking at American Holidays
Time: We the People
Communicative American English
English á la Cartoon

Text/Audiocassette Learning Packages
Speak Up! Sing Out!
Listen and Say It Right in English!

Transparencies
Everyday Situations in English

Duplicating Masters and
Black-line Masters
The Complete ESL/EFL Cooperative and
  Communicative Activity Book
Easy Vocabulary Games
Vocabulary Games
Advanced Vocabulary Games
Play and Practice!
Basic Vocabulary Builder
Practical Vocabulary Builder
Beginning Activities for English
  Language Learners
Intermediate Activities for English
  Language Learners
Advanced Activities for English
  Language Learners

Language-Skills Texts
Starting English with a Smile
English with a Smile
More English with a Smile
English Survival Series
  Building Vocabulary, Recognizing Details,
  Identifying Main Ideas, Writing Sentences
  and Paragraphs, Using the Context
English Across the Curriculum
Essentials of Reading and Writing English
Everyday English
Everyday Situations for Communicating in
  English
Learning to Listen in English
Listening to Communicate in English
Communication Skillbooks
Living in the U.S.A.
Basic English Vocabulary Builder Activity Book
Basic Everyday Spelling Workbook
Practical Everyday Spelling Workbook

Advanced Readings and Communicative
  Activities for Oral Proficiency
Practical English Writing Skills
Express Yourself in Written English
Campus English
English Communication Skills for Professionals
Speak English!
Read English!
Write English!
Orientation in American English
Building English Sentences
Grammar for Use
Grammar Step-by-Step
Listening by Doing
Reading by Doing
Speaking by Doing
Vocabulary by Doing
Writing by Doing
Look, Think and Write

Life- and Work-Skills Texts
English for Success
Building Real Life English Skills
Everyday Consumer English
Book of Forms
Essential Life Skills series
Finding a Job in the United States
English for Adult Living
Living in English
Prevocational English

TOEFL and University Preparation
NTC's Preparation Course for the TOEFL®
NTC's Practice Tests for the TOEFL®
How to Apply to American Colleges
  and Universities
The International Student's Guide
  to the American University

Dictionaries and References
ABC's of Languages and Linguistics
Everyday American English Dictionary
Building Dictionary Skills in
  English (workbook)
Beginner's Dictionary of American
  English Usage
Beginner's English Dictionary
  Workbook
NTC's American Idioms Dictionary
NTC's Dictionary of American Slang
  and Colloquial Expressions
NTC's Dictionary of Phrasal Verbs
NTC's Dictionary of Grammar Terminology
Essential American Idioms
Contemporary American Slang
Forbidden American English
101 American English Idioms
101 American English Proverbs
Practical Idioms
Essentials of English Grammar
The Complete ESL/EFL Resource Book
Safari Grammar
Safari Punctuation
303 Dumb Spelling Mistakes
TESOL Professional Anthologies
  Grammar and Composition
  Listening, Speaking, and Reading
  Culture

For further information or a current catalog, write:
National Textbook Company
a division of *NTC Publishing Group*
4255 West Touhy Avenue
Lincolnwood, Illinois 60646-1975 U.S.A.